SPROCKETS

The adventures of Juanita Yamashita

K.C. WANGMO

ISBN 978-1-950818-87-7 (paperback)
ISBN 978-1-950818-88-4 (digital)

Rushmore Press LLC
1 888 733 9607
www.rushmorepress.com

Printed in the United States of America

CONTENTS

PROLOGUE

Sprockets – a brief history

DOOMSDAY CAME AND went. The point of no-return to stem the tide of climate change passed almost unnoticed as the world chose to ignore rather than to act. Admittedly, folks were pretty busy with other stuff. While the planet was readjusting itself to the new normal, prolific advances in technology were creating the illusion that everything was going to be just fine.

The big event of course was our move into space with bases on the Moon, Mars and then space stations scattered throughout the asteroid belt. Man had finally escaped the constraints of a single planet. So, what was the urgency to tidy up the first one.

Much of that advance into the solar system was fostered by the inventions and innovations of one man. In 2042, Dr Raymond Mallard received the first of many patents for his sprockets technology based on twenty years of his research into rosehip neurons, first discovered in the early 2020s.

Nit everyone was a loser. There were indeed some big winners including most notably Canada. With the opening of the Northwest passage to year-around access and global warming transfrorming he frozen tundra of Alberta and Ottario provinces to breadbaskets for the rest of the world, Canada flourished.

2055

Virgin Gorda, Independent Commonwealth of Virgin Islands

CHAPTER 1

THE SUN WAS just extending itself over the horizon, as Juanita Yamashita, Nita to everyone except the Politz who came by checking papers every six months, pulled a light blue cotton shift over her tee shirt and panties. She slipped her feet into sandals and walked into the kitchen. This was her favorite time of day on the island. The breeze was cool and moist before the sweltering heat of afternoon set in. Her younger brothers, Jorge and Pepe, were still asleep, if they were home yet at all. Last night was a full moon and most likely they had spent a sizable amount of time at Bercher's Bay.

She stepped into the kitchen and smiled when she caught sight of the half pound of coffee sitting on the table where she had left it yesterday. Such a treat, along with the cream that was in the small fridge under the counter. But first to the morning chores. She collected the broom from the corner and began the slow, methodical process of sweeping out the single large room that comprised kitchen, dining room and living room.

When she was finished, she walked to the corner where the household shrines sat on two tables. Caring for her father's Shinto shrine only took a minute. The foreign gods had left just as quickly as her father when he departed less than a month after the death of her mother. She kept the shrine clean and a bowl of fresh water with a flower just in case her father ever returned and along with him, his gods.

It was her mother's shrine, and hers as well, that demanded her attention and respect. The Kalinago gods were very much present around her and in her. After cleaning and arranging the shrine offerings she sat on a small cushion at its base. First, she examined herself, assuring that her three souls of heart, head and shoulders were in harmony. All was well, all were cooperating. She then reached out her mind to Nonu-ma, the goddess of the moon, asking for protection, especially for her brothers who roamed so far away when her light was fullest. She next thanked her Icheiri for the bounty of her goat herd and the favorable weather and asked for his protection from the Mabouia who were so jealous of her good fortunes. In particular, she asked the Icheiri to intercede on her part with the local Boyez who still looked on her with such suspicion.

Her morning meditations complete, she walked out into the yard and to the chicken coop where she opened the door for her brood. They clucked at her as she sought out their gifts from the straw. She sighed. No eggs again from the two Wyandottes, who she was afraid were soon for the pot. The Plymouth Rocks on the other hand, were doing just fine. "Thank you, girls," she said as she pulled a half dozen eggs from the straw and deposited them in her basket.

It was just a short walk to the shed where she placed the eggs in the cooler. Next it was the milking pails that she grabbed and headed out to the goats whose bells she could already start hearing. It was going to be hard to face them today. Yesterday she had made her annual trip to The Valley to sell the eight bucklings from this year's breeding. There were only four females to keep this year, bringing her total of does up to fourteen. Within a year they would be giving milk making her herd a size too big for her to manage on her own. But she didn't have to make that decision right now.

The milking at last done, she took the pails back into the shed and placed them in the cooler. She checked the battery levels for the solar panels to make sure there was enough charge to keep the generator running until she could get the cheese made this afternoon. Otherwise, she would have to rouse her brothers to work the bikes. With the money from the sale of the kids yesterday, there was nearly enough to buy a new solar array with better battery life. Then she could start saving for a new, larger, cooler …

She was almost back to the kitchen when she smelled it. She almost fainted ... the stench. At the same time, she heard the voices of her brothers arguing about something from the front garden.

"I can't ... Pepe, she's too heavy. And when I try to move her, parts fall off." Jorge was fourteen and was the boss of his twelve-year-old younger brother. "Come-on, we got to get this behind the house before Nita sees."

Nita walked around to the front of the house and froze. Pepe and Jorge had definitely been to the dump last night. But what in the gods' names had they found? Her mouth formed a silent scream as she stared at what could only be guessed was a horribly decayed body twisted into her market wagon. Her first thought was to how she would get the wagon clean again to take her cheese and yogurt to The Valley and The Baths. Her second thought, still being formed, was even more unsettling.

It was then that Pepe and Jorge saw her. "Nita! You can't believe what we found! It's a fortune. We're going to be rich!" Jorge shouted.

On trembling legs, Nita cautiously walked up to the cart. She held her hand over her nose trying unsuccessfully to hold off the stench which Pepe and Jorge seemed to be oblivious to. Her eyes watered, and she thought she was going to throw up. She stared at Jorge, unable to process what he was saying.

"Jorge ..." she asked. She could now see that the corpse in her market wagon had once been a woman. Judging by the remaining tatters of clothing, a wealthy one at that.

"I'll explain later!" Jorge responded as he anxiously looked back towards the road. "We've got to get her behind the house and out of sight before anyone sees. I'll explain later."

Nina didn't know what else to do. Getting the body out of sight did seem to be the only thing that made any sense right now. She helped Jorge unhitch the wagon from their two bikes and then pull it up the hill to the back of the house where the chicken coop and goat sheds were located. The stench, if possible, was only getting worse.

They finally stopped when the wagon could go no farther in the rocky ground. Nita helped Jorge tip the body out of the wagon behind a few large boulders. She didn't know what horrified her more, the body lying on the ground or the ooze that was sinking into the floor boards of her cart. She turned to Jorge, looking for answers.

"It's sprockets! Don't you see? The shiny bits at her wrists … and look at the back of her head! We're rich!"

A tiny bit of understanding was building in Nita's mind. She listened as Jorge filled in the rest of the story.

"We found her at the dump last night, digging though a new section," he explained. "There was this huge new pile from two weeks ago. Everyone said it was cursed. There was a body there, they said. But Pepe and me, we didn't care. We saw it last night with everyone else. But I saw one of the sprockets too, so we came back early this morning and dragged her away. No one saw us, I swear."

"Look," he said as he used a stick to pull back the sleeve on the right arm and poke around until he could turn it over. And there it was, a sprocket port clearly visible with rotting flesh falling away from it.

Comprehension dawned for Nita. Sprocs. She, of course, had never seen one close up except for in the vids they showed during the cooler winter months in the Valley square. The few remaining tourists and the even fewer wealthy locals used theirs at the bank to jack in and make money transfers. But that was always from a discreet distance.

Questions filled her always sensible head. Were they still any good? And how did they get them out and cleaned up without destroying them if they were good? Where could they sell them? What if they got caught? Nina's mind began asking a thousand more questions even as she started building a plan to hide the body and see what would come next.

"Jorge," she asked. "Did anyone see you and Pepe take the body away?"

"No, Nita. That's why we left last night and then came back before first light this morning. We're going to tell everyone else that it must have been the authorities that took it away. Sprockets, Nita! Sprocs!"

Nita's plan began to form. "Jorge, Pepe, right now … tear the damaged boards out of the bottom of the cart. There are some old ones behind the chicken coop that you can use. Be careful. Make sure you get all the …" She wasn't sure what to call the vile ooze staining her wagon. "… bad bits," she continued. "Pepe, you go get some grass and some rock to cover the body, lots."

"When you're done," she added, unable to contain her growing feelings of optimism, "I'll make eggs for breakfast."

"Eggs! We're rich!" Jorge screamed as he ran towards the chicken coop.

Nita took a deep breath. How could someone be so terrified and excited at the same time? The gods of head and heart were in discord. She walked back to the shed and took this morning's six eggs from the cooler. Coffee and eggs … and a body. What had happened to her quiet morning?

She looked up at the sun now fully visible on the horizon. The stench of the rot of the body permeated each breath. How bad would it get in the full heat of the afternoon? Where was the quicklime? They would need it as soon as they figured out what to do.

* * * * *

Nita stood over the single electric burner waiting for the milk to come to just the edge of a boil. A large pot was on the counter draped with a piece of cheese cloth. Around her, everything was pristinely clean. This was the primary secret of her cheeses and yogurts that her customer's coveted. Yet in spite of all this preparation, she could still smell the rotting body. What if the stench got into her cheese? She shuddered at the thought.

It was good to finally be alone. The boys were quite understandably exhausted and now sleeping. Even the surprise of coffee with cream for breakfast couldn't keep them awake after the actions of the previous night and early morning.

She hoped she was doing the right thing. There was a rotting body of someone of importance hidden half-way up the hill. Shouldn't they contact someone? But who? What would they do but take the body away and claim the sprocs for themselves? It was no secret how the law worked and didn't work on the island. If you had money, there was law; if you didn't, well ...

It had taken a while for Nita to get the boys settled down over breakfast. First, she explained to them how they had to do nothing, absolutely nothing for at least three months to see what happened. Except of course, to harvest the sprocs. Nita didn't have any idea how the sprocs would respond to being embedded in the rotting corpse. Her sixth sense told her that it would be best to remove them now rather than later. She vaguely remembered a vid from a few years back of someone removing sprocs from their victim. How did they do it?

Over breakfast, she had reminded her two younger brothers to act as if nothing had happened. They were still to go to the dump a few times a week to see what they could collect. Absolutely, under no circumstances whatsoever, they were to tell anyone, not even their closest friends... Nor were they, as Pepe suggested, to go into the Valley to the kiosk and query anything about sprockets. Nothing had happened. Nothing.

For Nita, things would be a bit different. She poured the curdled goat's milk through the cheese cloth strainer and began squeezing out the whey. Patiently, she went through the ritual of cleaning her space, washing out pots and utensils. With so much milk today, it had taken eight separate batches and the cooler was completely full. Jars of yogurt lined the counter top. She knew without looking that the charge level on the solar panels was low. She was definitely going to need an additional solar array and a new cooler before the four does were ready to get knocked up by Mr. Billy and started to give milk later in the year.

With everything at last put away, she picked up the single slender knife that she used to carve her initials into the top of each cheese mold. She winced at the thought of using this precious piece of cutlery from her kitchen for something as disgusting as what she was about to do.

She looked around one final time and then, as an afterthought, picked up a piece of sacking from the corner. Closing the door behind her, she began the walk up the steep hillside. Pepe, to her surprise had done a great job of covering the body. Only the persistent smell gave away the location. It took Nita almost ten minutes to uncover one of the arms. By then, she was sweating and dirty from the exertion.

Cutting into flesh wasn't something either new or unsettling to Nina. There had been many times when she had to slaughter one of her does when it was old and no longer giving milk or had fallen and broken a leg. But this was different. For one thing, the flesh pulled away easily. For another, there was so much ooze that it was hard to see where her cuts were going. She started by trying to clear away the flesh around the port itself, resisting pulling on it. First, she wanted to see what the external surface of the port was connected to. What was on the underside of the sprocket? She had no idea what to expect.

Patiently, she peeled and cut back flesh. As she did so, she wished she had brought a bucket of water to help wash away the ooze. As best as she could tell, the sprocket trailed six or so fine filaments a few inches into what remained of the muscle of the arm. When she at last had the port fully exposed, she used the tip of her knife to pull the port gently up and into the air, separating it completely from the arm.

She looked at it, not really sure what she had in front of her. Was there anything else that she was missing that was still embedded in the arm? Carefully, she put the two-inch long apparatus on the piece of sackcloth. With her knife again, she returned to the arm and began pulling back skin and muscles, looking to see if there was anything she had missed. Satisfied that there was nothing else that could be salvaged, she went about uncovering the other arm and repeating the process.

It went smoother and faster this time as she knew where to cut and what the port looked like. It was when she started the process of removing the port on the back of this poor woman's neck however that she had to stop and figure out what to do. Neck ports, she remembered from the vids, were special. Most people, even when they could afford it, only had wrist sprockets. It was only the techs, and other super important people who had neck ports – and spies too. This is where they could send, store, and receive massive amounts of data.

Then she remembered. Wasn't there also a chip, a thin sliver of tech embedded somewhere behind the port? She hadn't been to a vid in years and her memory was foggy. The port came loose much the way that the other two ports had done. Again, it had half a dozen or so thin wires dangling from it. There was a slight difference, however. Each of the tiny wires on this port had a minuscule knob on the end. Nina took her slender knife and poked carefully under the back of the skull, seeing if she could make contact with anything that felt hard.

Her knife blade was about two inches in when she thought she felt something. She pulled the knife tip out and then made a decision. Grimacing, she carefully, pushed her thumb and forefinger into the space behind the base of the skull. In just a few seconds she found what she was looking for. It took some more pushing of oozing flesh before she could get it between her two fingers. When she pulled, it slipped out easily, slimy and dripping. It was less than an inch in length and incredibly thin. She held it up into the departing sunlight to get a better look.

The angle of the sun surprised her. It had taken up the better part of the afternoon to extract the tech and she hadn't even started any dinner for her two brothers. There was millet to cook, squashes to get from the garden .... She tried not to rush as she carefully folded the sprockets into the burlap and then just as carefully, re-covered the body. She shuddered at the risk she and her brothers were taking. If anyone ever found this body, they would know that there had once been tech and now it was gone. But then the possibility of rewards overcame her fears. A new solar array, a new cooler ....

CHAPTER 2

The next three months were the longest of Nita's seventeen years of life. The tech, now as pristinely clean as Nita's cheese-making platform, was wrapped in cheese cloth, hidden in the rafters of the chicken coop. The boys had dug a proper grave high up on the side of the hill and deposited what was left of the body. It had taken several trips to collect all the bits that were falling off as the decay continued.

Nothing was said between them - not even during meals in the kitchen - about what had happened. Nita continued to make her weekly trips to the Baths and to the Valley to sell her cheese and yogurt; the boys continued their trips to the dump. Life continued as usual.

After the three months were over and nothing had turned up in any of the local and national feeds at the kiosk about a missing girl, Nita and her brothers began to feel that it might be safe to talk about what they wanted to do next. Nita, of course, wanted to sell the tech exactly as it was, working or not. But Jorge and Pepe had a different idea. Why didn't Nita get jacked herself? Jorge and Pepe, like all boys their ages who were otherwise healthy, planned to enter the military as soon as they were of age. Military service was the easiest way to get jacked. Five years of service got you jacked; ten got you upgrades that you got to keep after you got out – assuming that you lived that long. Neither Jorge or Pepe knew of anyone who had gotten out with their tech. but then, they reasoned, if you had tech why would you come back to the island.

Nita, being a girl, was excluded from that path. It wasn't that the military was against girls signing up; it was just, with the promises of tech, that so many young boys were signing up that they didn't need girls any more. There was only one other path for girls who were born without a silver spoon in their mouth to acquire tech – and that was the oldest trade in the world.

Nita began making cautious inquiries at the Baths while she was selling cheese and yogurt. There was a time when the dinghies that pulled up to the shore were full of wealthy tourists and the sycophants of massively wealthy industrialists whose yachts sat at anchor off shore. Now, however, increasingly, the yachts offshore were those of the profiteers who had once again made the Caribbean the stronghold of pirates and other miscreants.

One of those men, who Nita assumed was one of the pirates, stood in front of her now alternating his stare between the cheeses and the neckline of her dress. His sprockets were plainly visible on the inside of his wrists, especially so, given that they were the only clean areas on his entire body. He was a regular customer, so she decided to take a chance. With what she imagined to be doleful eyes, she confessed how she dreamed of having sprockets too, no matter what it would take. "Wasn't there anything that a girl could do to get her very own sprockets like his, just the simplest of types, really?"

She had second thoughts, however, when the man leaned forward over the table and put a hand on her shoulder. She could smell the sourness of his breath and pulled her head back in disgust.

He laughed. "There are of course always ways that a pretty girl like you can get jacked," he said, and then added with a laugh, "… eventually, of course."

It took every ounce of her courage to continue the conversation. "And where," she asked, "… could a girl get jacked, assuming she could afford it?" She was shocked, even after she pushed his hand off her shoulder in clear rejection, when he actually gave her the names of two shops in Road Town.

He'd walked away then, stuffing one of her cheeses in his mouth, laughing. "But it's going to take more than you can make selling cheese, that's for sure," he shouted over his shoulder.

"And especially if you don't pay for them," she had muttered under her breath. But at least she now had the names of two places where they could start their efforts to off-load the tech.

* * * * *

"Nita," Jorge explained between mouths of stew. "There's a place in Road Town where this guy works with bogo tech. He can jack you for sure."

"Why can't we just sell him the tech?" Nita asked, wondering how Jorge had acquired his information, nervous again that their secret might get out. She hadn't shared yet the names she had acquired in her own ways and was wondering if their stories matched.

"Sis," Jorge said with eyes that betrayed a life of experiences far greater than his years. "We aren't going to be around forever," he turned to Pepe who nodded in agreement. "We got to get you taken care of too."

"But I'd be scared to death. I thought this stuff was matched to whoever it is jacked to." Nina nervously explained, even though she felt an unexpected tingle of hope.

"Nah, this guy in Road Town knows how to fix that, least that's what we've been told."

Now Nita was nervous. Who had they been talking to? Wouldn't someone be suspicious if they were both asking around? "What's his name?" she asked.

Nita was relieved when one of the names matched the list she had acquired in her own way. "Enrico's," she said, deciding for them. "That's a name that I heard too."

"Then come on, Nita, let's get a boat to Road Town and get you jacked. Even if it doesn't work, they can unjack you again and we can still sell it for whatever we could have got initially." Jorge was on his feet, ready to leave that very instant and then stopped when he realized that Nita was still sitting at the kitchen table.

Eventually, they opted to wait until the following Tuesday morning to get the first boat out of the harbor. It was going to be expensive and Nita felt a tinge of concern. She would also have to make different arrangements with her new assistant, Carmine, who for the past month had been coming to the house every day to help milk the goats and make yogurt. And this was Nita's dilemma. She still kept her cheese recipe a secret and always shooed Carmine out of the shed when she did her preparations. Could she trust Carmine with her recipe while they were gone? No, she decided. It would just be a day, maybe two, that they would be gone. Carmine could make yogurt for a day and they could turn it into cheese later.

*****

Over the next few days they prepared. Jorge found a boat to Road Town that didn't ask too many questions and Nita painfully gave up her hard-won savings to pay for their passage huddled in the bow to avoid any curious on-lookers. Nita insisted on paying in advance for round-trip passage which surprised the boat owner. Few who could afford the passage to the big island of Tortola wanted to come back to Virgin Gorda. With the fishing and tourist industries gone, the only industries remaining on the island were limited to supporting the needs of the privateers. Anyone with any ambition at all knew that the only opportunities were on Tortola.

Gratefully, the sea was calm, and they made it across Drake channel without event. The sun was barely up when they off-boarded and checked with the captain for the approximate time for his return trip. Minutes later they were walking through the winding streets of Road Town. As they went, they continued to build their story, rehearsing down to the smallest details. They decided that Jorge, given his superior knowledge of Road Town, would initially do the talking. Jorge had started making trips to Road Town two years earlier with a half-dozen older boys. They brought the pickings from the dump, once junk not worth saving, but now precious commodities, especially metals and pieces of ancient tech with their precious metal conductors, to the resellers on the big island. He knew his way around. Or so his story went.

Through a process of trial and error, they eventually found the shop just off an alley, off another alley. Neither the alley nor the shop had a name, Jorge did the talking.

"We found this dead tourist person, see, washed up on the beach. Most likely from one of the boats off the shore at the Baths." Jorge lied with an ease that made Nita wonder about any additional hidden skills of her younger brother. "Pretty messed up … not sure if they work or not, ocean water and all." Jorge shrugged his shoulders as if to say, there's not much here – of course, unless there was.

Even as the three children stood in front of the counter, waiting for a response, their eyes wandered hungrily around the shop. There was tech everywhere. Nita, not being a tech-head the way that her brothers were, was at a complete loss as to what she was looking at. Jorge, however, kept nodding appreciatively as his eyes caught sight of each gadget.

"Now let me get this straight," the strange man behind the counter said. He pushed back what remained of wispy thin blonde hair from his face. "You want me to put this tech into this island girl here, your sister, right, not knowing if it works or not, not knowing what it is or where it comes from?"

Nita gulped and then silently nodded her head up and down in lieu of the word that escaped her. She couldn't take her eyes off the tats that ran up and down both of his exposed arms, up his neck, and onto the sides of his face.

"So how you gonna pay?" The man's eyes turned to Nita, looking her up and down in a way that made Nita's skin crawl. Jorge quickly stepped forward and stood between Nita and the man at the counter. "Not that," he said with a level of authority that didn't match his stature.

"Okay, then what? What have you kids got that I don't already have three of?" The man rolled his eyes towards the shelves covered with tech. He turned his wrists over, revealing three ports on each arm, just for emphasis.

"What do you want?" Jorge asked cautiously. "We need a price if they work and one if they don't work."

The man scratched the back of his neck where Nita guessed he had another port. She wondered why he needed so many ports.

"Okay … here's the deal." He looked first at Jorge and Pepe and then stared for an extensive time at Nita. "I put the tech in, right, but no guarantees. If it doesn't work, then you give me the tech as a payment for services rendered." He paused, looking at each of the kids one after another.

"However, … If it does work, then we've got another deal. One of you, I'm thinking maybe this pretty young thing," he leered at Nita again. "… works for me, for …" he paused to think a bit. "… say, six months, to pay off the debt for jacking her."

"What kind of work?" Jorge asked suspiciously. He looked back and forth between Nita and the increasingly menacing-looking man behind the counter.

"Well, if the ports are working, then there's lots of work that I can think of, some research, say …"

Nita pushed Jorge aside and stepped up to stand directly in front of the man. "What kind of work? Be specific."

"Well, so the little lady finally speaks." The man grinned, revealing a mouth full of multi-colored teeth. "What kind … well, we'll definitely think of something. With that tri-port you got there, there's lots and lots I can have you do."

Nita took a half step back and dropped her head. "We need to think about it a bit." She nodded at Jorge and Pepe to follow her as she quickly turned and backed out of the shop into the narrow alley.

She grabbed both of her brothers by the shoulders and huddled down with their heads together. "So, what do you think?" she asked, even though she had already made up her own mind.

"Look," she explained. "Its no big deal. I've got to learn how to use the tech anyway. So, let's just think of it being, like I'm going to school for six months. Right?" She knew the lie of what she was saying, but in a rush, she realized how much she wanted this, really wanted this.

"Nita, I don't know …" Jorge was shaking his head.

Nita had a thought. "Why don't we bargain for some tech for both of you, something off the shelves in there?"

She had them. Both Jorge and Pepe lifted their heads and grinned. As much as they loved their sister, this was far too tempting.

When they returned to the shop, it was Nita who took over the negotiation. "Okay, it's a deal," she said. "But I want something for my brothers too. After all, they're the ones who found the body."

It was a matter then of bartering, just the way she did at the market. While she negotiated, Jorge and Pepe walked around the shop standing on tip toe to see everything that was on display, their eyes popping out of their heads.

Nita had a flash of insight. "Not this stuff," she waved her hand toward the shelves. "What do you have in the back? Where's the good stuff?"

The man smiled, revealing his rainbow-colored mouth again. It was clear to Nita that he really wanted to make this deal.

"Just a minute, I've got just the thing for them," he said, and turned to disappear into a back room. Nita caught a glimpse of what else was in the back room. She could see a chair, just like the ones in the vids, with lots of metal wires and posts hovering over it. She shuddered. But it was too late to back out now.

Simultaneously, Jorge and Pepe came back to the counter as the man also came back to the counter. Jorge put a small box on the counter along with an antique headset. The man gave a snort, pushed their box aside and put a similar, but in decidedly much better condition, box and headset on the counter. Both Jorge's and Pepe's eyes got wide in recognition.

"What is it?" Nina asked.

"It's a G-glass console, a G-cube." Jorge whispered, his awe transparent as he stared wide-eyed at the top of the counter. He gasped then as the man pulled open a carton of at least 100 filaments and tipped the contents onto the counter.

"We sometimes get to use them at class," Jorge explained breathlessly. Pepe nodded his head in agreement. "But we only have one set for the whole school."

"Looks like we have a deal, then." Nita reached out her hand across the counter to seal the relationship. The man's hand felt unsettlingly oily.

*****

Nita lost track of time as she sat in the chair. To her relief, it seemed that everything was automated. The wrist sprockets were first. She put her arms, wrist side up, in the slots on either side of the chair. She wasn't sure if it was minutes or hours before she looked down again and saw the red puckered skin around each small port. They were smaller than she expected, barely the size of a bean.

"Sweet, huh," the man said, guessing what she was thinking. "That's some really impressive tech you kids found. Not sure if I've seen anything this small before. Got to be the latest thing."

Jorge and Pepe stepped up and looked down at their sister's wrists. "Wow! This is so …" Jorge paused and looked up at the man. His face asked the question before the words came out.

"Do they work?" Is that what you want to know?" the man finished their thoughts. "Looks like it. You feel anything? Like a tingle or something?" he asked Nita.

Nita paused, trying to get a sense of how she was feeling. Everything was still in a fog as a result of the sticky sweet syrup the man, whose name it turned out was indeed Ernesto, gave her before they started. Yes, there it was. Just a faint tingle, almost like her hands had fallen asleep and circulation was returning. She wasn't quite sure how much to reveal. "A bit, I think, kind of tingling."

"Yup. That's it." He said, smiling again in a way that continued to unsettle Nita.

"That's easy, now the hard part." Ernesto, or Ernie as he insisted on being called, reached out and quickly tilted the chair that Nita was strapped into forward. Without warning, he grabbed the back of her neck and pushed her even further forward until she was in a curled-up position looking down at the floor. All in the same motion, she felt straps wrapping around her shoulders and across the top of her head. She wanted to scream, but there was no air in her lungs.

"Real pity you kids didn't get the chip." Ernie shook his head in disgust as he pulled Nita's hair back and daubed something orange along her hairline. "Now that would be a real bonus. You were probably too dumb to know where to find it and take it out. Guess I'll have to find a blank one and charge you an extra, hmmm … month for formatting it."

Nina hesitated and then made a decision. "Jorge," she said in a mumbled voice. "Get my shawl. There's a patch at the bottom. Pull it apart – be careful."

Jorge collected Nina's shawl from the front of the shop and then returned to stand next to the chair, looking at her nervously. "You okay, Nita? That looks really uncomfortable."

"Just give it to him," she gasped, "Hurry."

Ernie smiled again. "Well aren't you just a bundle of surprises." He pulled out a pair of tweezers from somewhere out of Nita's limited range of sight and reached over her to pull the thin sliver of silicon from the edge of the shawl.

"What's he doing?" Nita asked, as she struggled to loosen the straps around her head and shoulders.

"He's got this THING he's holding. He's …" Jorge didn't get a chance to finish his description before Nita screamed. And then she screamed again and again, before her entire body went slack.

"What's happened?" Jorge screamed on his own account. Pepe. too, came rushing up to see what was happening.

"Nah, kids, relax. She isn't dead. Least I don't think so. The chip's integrating with her brain stem. She'll come out in a few minutes and then we can take a look and see what we've got." Having said that, Ernie began loosening all the straps holding Nita in place. With a tenderness that registered as shock on both Jorge's and Pepe's faces, he picked up her limp body and carried her to an out of place green velvet couch against the wall.

"She'll be coming out any minute now, he reassured the two boys who were crowding behind him. "Damnest tech I've ever seen for a quite some time. Just about jacked itself, like it knew where it was supposed to be going." Ernie shook his head and then walked across the room to a refrigeration unit. "Cokes?" he asked.

Jorge and Pepe both nodded their heads in enthusiastic agreement. Cokes. Today was really like Christmas. At least for them. For Nita, neither of them was sure. She hadn't moved an inch since Ernie had jacked her.

* * * * *

It wasn't minutes, it wasn't even a half hour. It was over four hours before Nita at last returned to consciousness. During that time, Ernie's nervousness increased exponentially as he alternated between pacing the floor in the back office and then again in the front of the shop. Sometime after the first hour of Nita's unconsciousness, he had walked into the shop and shuttered all the windows and locked the doors. Jorge and Pepe didn't notice. They were far too absorbed sharing turns with the G-Cube.

Awareness came slowly for Nita. Was it a dream or was she awake? And who was she? There was so much going through her mind right now. Fragments of memories of a life that she had never lived. Emotional responses to memories that weren't hers. She kept her eyes closed, remaining as still as possible as she tried to push down the panic she was feeling. Gradually she became aware of her surroundings. There were voices of Jorge and Pepe, occasional movement of who she assumed was the man called Ernie. She was no longer in the chair, no longer tied down, but was lying on something very soft and comfortable.

But there was something else too. Another voice in her head, not loud, just murmuring in the background. It must be the chip, she guessed. With both excitement and fear she realized that the tech was working. She could feel it waiting in the background. But what next?

She opened her eyes, keeping her head still. She was in the same room where Ernie had installed her ports. But she wasn't. She sought for words to describe what she was seeing, feeling. The room was alive, vibrant, each color and shadow leaping out at her. It must be the chip, the chip ....

"Hey, she's back! Her eyes are open!" Jorge jumped up and ran to the couch. "Sis, are you okay?"

Jorge's face looking down at her was the most beautiful thing she had ever seen. Why had she never noticed what a handsome young man her brother was? It brought a smile to her face.

"Sis, come on, say something," Jorge pleaded. "Are you okay?"

Ernie heard the sound of Jorge's voice and came back into the room. He took one look at Nita and pushed past Jorge to wrap Nita's head in both of his hands, turning it back and forth.

"I'm okay. Stop please," she said as she resisted Ernie's efforts to twist her neck. The words echoed in her head. Even his touch was something she had never felt before. Her skin was on fire. She put her hands on the couch and pushed herself to a seated position. The velvet of the fabric tingled in her palms.

"Okay," Ernie said as he took a half-step back. "So, what are you feeling? Is anything going on for you?"

"Yeah, I guess," she said cautiously, suddenly aware that it might not be the best idea to tell Ernie everything that she was experiencing. "Things seem a bit brighter," she said, trying to make her voice far less excited than she was feeling, "And there's a hum in the background like music drifting up from the beach. Is that okay?"

"Well I'll be damned. You kids really hit the jackpot. Me too, it seems. Damn." Ernie scratched his head and grinned, revealing his rainbow-colored mouth.

"You think you can get up so we can jack you in and see what we've got?"

"I think so," Nita said, swinging her legs around until her feet were on the floor. The coolness of the tile sent a thrill through her legs and up her spine. Everything was so alive. And so was her bladder.

"I've got to pee," she said matter of factly. "Where's the toilet?"

"Uhh, yeah, over there." Ernie stepped back again and pointed to a door at the back of the room.

Nita followed him with her eyes and then pushed herself up from the couch. It felt so new to her, just standing, doing nothing but standing motionless in one place. She desperately didn't want Ernie to know what she was experiencing. Every fiber of her being, joined by the chorus of voices and memories that continued to invade her consciousness, cautioned her to minimize the information she gave him.

"Be right back," she mumbled and then slowly took the first steps of her new life hoping that her wobbliness would be credited to the aftereffects of being jacked and not to the fact that she felt that she was learning to walk for the first time.

Time passed. Without being aware of the last few minutes, Nita found herself standing in front of the cracked mirror over the sink fascinated by her own reflection. She couldn't remember the last five minutes. But memories, not hers, and from untold times in the past, were fresh in the front of her consciousness as if they had just happened. She stared at herself as if looking into the face of a stranger. Only the sound of water splashing over the rim of the sink and onto the floor broke her out of her trance. Quickly she reached down and closed the taps and pulled the rusted chain attached to the drain plug.

When she returned to the room, Ernie and her two brothers were standing next to a table with a massive screen in its middle. Apart from the overall griminess of the surroundings, it reminded Nita of scenes from the Friday night vids in the Valley. Ernie was holding the end of a bluish thin cable, barely more than a thread, and looking at her with far more eagerness than she felt comfortable with. One end was already connected to the screen. The other end, pinched between his fingers, was clearly intended for Nita.

She took a deep breath. There was no going back now. She didn't even know where 'back' was anymore. As much out of fear and the fact that she still wasn't sure of her own steps, she slowly and cautiously walked towards the table and the chair in front of it. Every time she put a foot down, a flood of sensation poured through her. It took every ounce of effort to reach the chair and sit down.

"Still dizzy, huh?" he asked, and then put his hand on Nita's head and pushed it forward to get access to the port at the base of her neck. "Some folks feel that way, others not so much," Ernie explained, as he pushed aside the rest of her hair and inserted the connector into her port.

Nita gasped. And so did Ernie. And then Jorge and Pepe. Nita quickly raised her head and stared at the screen. At first it was hard to figure out what she was looking at. The initials NAA-BI filled half of the screen with a picture of a bird of some kind shadowed behind. The next thing she noticed were the words *Connecting ...* across the bottom. And then it went blank just as she felt a tug as the connector was yanked from her neck.

"You bitch! What the fuck!" Ernie swiveled the chair around and pushed so hard that Nita fell to the floor. "Get out!" he screamed, as he started kicking her. "All of you, get out!"

Nita looked up to see pure terror in Ernie's eyes. She scrambled to her feet, trying to avoid his kicks. The task was more difficult that it should be. The same display that had been on the screen was overlaying her vision. It was as if the screen was inside her head while at the same time she could still see what was otherwise in front of her. The word *connected* was blinking in the right-hand corner of her vision. Something was horribly wrong.

Ernie was still screaming, and if possible, still more desperate looking. "You're a pol, a goddamn pol!" he screamed. "For god's sake get out!"

Jorge saved the day. He grabbed Nita by the arm and began pushing her towards the door to the front of the shop. Pepe was already there at the outer door, holding the G-cube and box of films in his hands.

"Wait," Nita yelled, following a direction from the other voice in her head. She reached back and grabbed the bluish cable yanking it free from the screen. Immediately it curled into a small coil that fit in the palm of her hand.

"Okay. Let's go!" she yelled even more forcefully, following the insistent voices in her head. In a few steps she was at the front of the shop where her bag and shawl were draped across a chair. She grabbed both and ran to the door – which was locked. Jorge was alternatingly tugging on the handle and pounding on the wall next to the door.

"Open it!" she screamed, now just as terrified as Ernie. She wasn't sure if Ernie had done something or if Jorge's pounding had found a switch. But as soon as the words left her mouth the door clicked and swung outward to reveal a pitch-black night. *How long had they been there?* Nita wondered as she ran along with her two brothers down the alley.

* * * * *

The first light of morning was just showing on the horizon as Jorge led his brother and sister to the water's edge. He seemed to know what he was looking for. He guided both of them to a half turned over boat with its side propped open with a large stick. Quickly he ducked under the side of the boat and motioned Nita and Pepe to follow him. There was just enough space for the three of them to sit closely together and most importantly, completely out of sight from the road.

Nita couldn't stop shaking. The picture from the screen in the shop was still overlaying her vision. There was an additional blinking light above the *connected* message. She looked at Jorge, trying to draw some reassurance from him.

"What just happened?" she asked, hoping that he understood better than her the events of the last twelve hours.

"What happened?" he said and turned to her with a huge grin. "We just bested him, that's what. We've got tech. You've got sprockets. And it didn't cost us a pound. That was outrageous!" Jorge wrapped his arms around his sister and gave her a hug.

"But why did he throw us out? Something really, really scared him." Nita asked, trying to keep her voice as empty of content as possible. She wasn't quite ready to share with her brothers what was going on inside her head. Her heightened senses continued to startle her. In the darkness underneath the boat she could make out Jorge and Pepe as is they were in broad daylight. Every caulked crack and beam stood out in crystal clarity. Her own terror spiked as the thought occurred to her that these sensations might never go away. Could she ever get used to them and accept them as normal?

"We've got to get a boat back home, that's for sure." Jorge said in a calm, confident tone. Nita suspected that it was just a front and

Jorge was probably just as terrified as she was. But she didn't care. She would believe what she needed to believe, in order to survive.

Jorge reached down and picked up Nita's shopping bag. "I'll need about ten pounds to book us a boat back to the Valley – okay?"

"Okay," she said and reached into the bag Jorge was holding to pull out her wallet. She felt relief that he would quickly be gone, and she could avoid describing what was going on inside her head. What had happened and what was NAA-BI?

CHAPTER 3

Mike ran past the protesting receptionist and into the director's office, gasping for air. It had been many years since he was built for running.

"Boss, you're not going to believe this!" He skidded to a stop in front of the desk and then at the last moment realized that there was already someone in Director Frank Walker's office.

"Sorry!" he said, "Geez, we've gotta talk, like right now." How could he make the director know how important this was?

Director Walker scowled, but then paused, perhaps realizing that Mike's outburst was the exception, not the rule to his senior analyst's behavior.

"Okay, Mike," he explained as he leaned forward and put his clasped hands patiently on the desk. "Whatever it is, you can talk in front of Mary. She's our liaison with the North American Alliance Oversight Committee."

Mike paused, wondering if revealing to this politician what he had discovered was truly a good idea. But there was no time for second guessing. Any minute now they might lose the signal and Julia, dear Julia, could be gone for good.

"Okay, It's Julia," he explained, still out of breath. "She just came on line, actually still online. Someplace in the Virgin islands of all places."

Director Walker's face lit up. He half-stood behind his desk. "You're absolutely sure its Julia?"

"Yeah, it's her call signal. Though she hasn't responded except for the first connect. She's probably in trouble."

"Good God! If you're right, then we need to act fast." Director Walker was halfway around his desk before he remembered that he was not the only person in the room. "Mary," he explained, as he continued to walk to the door, leaving her still seated in front of the desk. "I've got to attend to this. We'll have to catch up later." Director Walker quickly walked to the door followed by Mike. He didn't wait to hear Mary's response.

"Most expensive tech we've ever developed … caught hell for losing it," he shouted over his shoulder as he rapidly retraced Mike's steps back to the research lab. Mike, still struggling to catch his breath, ran behind him.

"Came in around five this morning. Just out of the blue. I've got a trigger mapped to her IP and that's how I found it. Got here in record time to see it on the lab console, not sure it might be a glitch in my sprocs." Mike wasn't sure that Director Walker was hearing him as he spoke to the Director's back.

"Just show me." Director Walker said as he walked into the lab. Julia was the prize possession of the NAA-BI research division. Top, top, and top again, secret and literally millions, if not billions, into her development. And his too, but that was another untold story. When she had gone missing six months ago, everyone, including himself assumed the worst. The blowback had been hell.

"Here," Mike said and pointed to one of the screens in the middle of the room. There were already half a dozen analyst's either sitting or standing in front of it.

"Is she still on line?" Mike asked.

"Yeah," one of the analysts said. "But its really weird. She's not responding to any of our pings. She's just hanging there with an open line. Real strange, if it's really Julia."

Director Walker shoved one of the techs sitting directly in front of the screen out of his chair and replaced him in directly in front of the blinking display. He quickly drew a thin bluish cable from his pocket and jacked it into the screen and then into the port on the back of his neck.

Mike and the rest of the analysts watched in awe as their boss gave non-verbal commands that caused two other windows to come up beside the one with Julia's call information. It was biometric data. Mike recognized Julia's data, but the other set, while similar, and supposedly coming live from Julia's chip was something new. Mike wondered how Walker was getting what was clearly an active download. *Did Director Walker have a chip like Julia's?*

"Well its not Julia," Director Walker concluded, sitting back in the chair. "It's definitely Julia's tech, and its live, but it's not Julia who's jacked in. Look ...." He pointed at several sine waves displayed on the left side of the screen. "Pulse, blood pressure .... all different."

Everyone seated or standing remained motionless as they waited for the director to say something else.

"Whatever or whoever this is," he said after a moment of reflection. "We've got to get it back, and right now. Mike, get a team together and build a plan." Director Walker turned around and looked at Mike as if he were seeing him for the first time.

"Boss, that's out of our jurisdiction. We've got no leverage there – its just a bunch of modern-day pirates."

It was true, the Virgin Island, both the American and British, about 20 years ago had decided to go it on their own, and self-proclaim themselves to be the Independent Commonwealth of Virgin Islands or ICVI for short. . With the tourist trade having all but disappeared due to the exorbitant cost of travel, given the depletion of fuel sources, the islands had returned to their original, and by far most profitable, revenue stream – privateering.

"I could give a rat's ass," Director Walker exclaimed. "Get down there now and get my tech back – or don't bother to come back at all!"

* * * * *

The doors and shutters were all locked down tight. All his tech was turned off at the mains. Not a single light blinked anywhere except the one single green light on the solar fueled generator. Ernie sat in total darkness thinking about all the ways that his life was truly fracked. Damn and double damn, how had those kids fooled him? He could have sworn that they were stupid, yes, but on the up and up. What had happened?

Ernie knew it was time to do what he had to do and desperately dreaded. He hit the flashlight button on his phone and crawled over to the desk and from memory keyed in the code that opened the bottom right drawer. The small phone resting by itself at the bottom of the drawer looked innocent enough. But Ernie knew better. He sighed and then picked up the phone and hit the screen for the single number in the address book.

After only two rings, it picked up and the sound of soft breathing came from the other end of the line. "Boss, I've got problems, big fracking problems."

"Okay, go on." The voice on the other side was barely more than a whisper.

"It's kids, came in with some outa sight sprocs, tri-port, said they got them off a body on the beach." Ernie paused, giving the person on the other end time to respond. When no response came, he continued. "Got this fine young girl, just a kid, jacked. Thought I could use her for the next six months, like for some odd jobs ..."

"Get to the point," the voice interrupted.

"Okay," Ernie could feel sweat dripping under his arms and down his back. "I got her jacked into a screen and as soon as it came on-line, there's a screen with NAA-BI in huge letters and a message saying that we were connecting to somewhere. Scared me shitless."

There was a pause, was the boss still there? But Ernie could hear the breathing, just the same slow in and out.

"Where is she now?" the voice asked in the same monotone.

"Hell if I know," Ernie said a lot louder than he intended. "I unjacked her as quick as I could and sent them out the door. I'm completely shut down, shuttered, off-line. I've gone dark."

The voice from the other end of the line was silent again. If anything, the in and out of the breathing sounded slower than before.

It felt like a minute before the response came back, still in its whisper-like tones but with an overlay of intensity. "You are a fracking idiot." There was a pause again. "You are to find her, do you understand, now, and you are to obtain the tech. I don't care if the container is in pieces. In fact, pieces would be my preference. When you have it, in whatever state you choose, you are to wait for my people to pick it up. This number will be deactivated."

Ernie waited for any additional instructions. He realized that the sound of breathing was no longer there. The line was dead.

*****

Jorge came back to the turned over boat in less than an hour. He peeked inside to where he saw Nita resting back against the inside of the boat hull with Pepe's head in her lap, sound asleep. He took a quick look around to see if there was anyone watching and then ducked under the edge of the boat.

"Found someone." he whispered. Pepe raised his head and rubbed his eyes.

Surprisingly, Nita was wide awake. But then of course she had the four hours of being unconscious.

"He's leaving in about an hour from pier four. Taking some …"

"Shhh…" Nita whispered in her brothers' ear and pulled her two brothers closer to her under the boat hull, putting her finger to her mouth indicating silence.

A few moments later, footsteps came through the boat yard accompanied by a conversation between a group of men.

"Damn, where could those kids be? Ernie said three of them. Some hot girl with long black curly hair and two smaller boys."

"Shit, they're probably off the island by now." Another voice chimed in.

"How's that? Who gets off this island these days unless they already had a way on?"

"Anyone say where they came from? They live somewhere on the island?"

"Ernie said they found a body on a beach somewhere so I'm guessing its up on the north side. Tide's heavier there."

The group stopped just outside the perimeter of the overturned boat. Nita could see broken down boots positioned just a foot or two outside the edge of the boat.

"Then why the hell are we looking here? Let's go North and see if someone knows about them."

"Well, we better do it fast. Ernie is in one right fit that we find them, her at least. Something about some stolen tech he wants back."

The voices drifted away. Jorge squirmed under Nita's left arm as she realized that she was hugging each of her brothers in intense arm locks. "Sorry," she whispered into Jorge's ear and kissed him on the head. "Let's wait half an hour and then head for the pier."

Nita added one more line to the growing list of strange things happening to her body. She had picked up an internal clock, an extremely precise one, she realized. Exactly half an hour later, she sent Jorge and Pepe out to find the boat. They decided that it would be best if they didn't move around together as a threesome. No one would pay too much attention to two boys roaming around the boat yard, nor, hopefully, too much attention to a woman with her head wrapped in a shawl and a young boy.

Their plan worked, and, after paying an exorbitant amount to the boat owner, they were headed back across the seventeen miles ocean span to Spanish Town and the Valley. Nita spent the trip crouched in the bow, as much hiding, as reflecting on the last twenty-four hours of her life. Her senses remained overloaded. The sound of the waves slapping against the bow, the rumble of the motor, the wind ripping through the canvas tarps … all of it was too much.

Biting her lower lip, she held back her tears. She had to be strong for Jorge and Pepe even though she was scared out of her wits. She knew that even though they were heading back to the relative safety of their home, there was no real safety, not for long at least. It was only a matter of time before they were tracked down.

And she knew what she had to do. When the time came, she would no longer resist. She would go with them, buying time and safety for her two brothers. They had made a horrible mistake in retrieving the tech, but it was too late to change that now. Even now, curled up with her arms wrapped around her knees, she could sense how it was biting into her, how it was becoming harder and harder to separate the dreams from reality. When she had dozed off in the midday heat under the boat hull, the dreams immediately started. Not the shadowy dreams of midnight, but full color, more real than reality. Places, faces of people, buildings, all a jumble, none of it making any sense, but leaving her with memories as real as her own. It was getting hard to know who she was.

Silently, she called on the gods of her mother to help her. She reached out her mind to Nonu-ma, the goddess of the moon, asking for protection from whatever dangers lay ahead for her and her brothers. She made sure to thank her Icheiri for the bounteous gift of these sprockets and asked them as well for their protection. As she did so, she felt their presence in a way that was new to her. The words of her mother from so long ago came to her.

> *When you become a woman, the gods will speak to you in a different voice, Nita. And you will be able to speak back to them. Forget what the Boyz say about their supposed unique relationship with the gods. My mother and my mother's mother's through all of time have had the gift. I believe, even though you have your father's blood as well, that you will have the same gift. When it comes, welcome it with open arms. Surrender to it completely.*

Huddled in the bow of the boat, she missed her mother terribly. She felt so all alone. And yet at the same time she felt herself to be amidst so many, many voices. Her mother had said 'surrender'.

Letting herself be rhythmically rocked by the movement of the boat, she let her mind match the patterns of the water. She let her mind float on the waves of thoughts and emotions – the memories, the new insights, the connections that continued to weave through her awareness as various parts of her being introduced themselves to each other as if for the first time – she surrendered to whatever direction they were taking her. At some level, she knew her life depended on it.

CHAPTER 4

NITA WOKE AT her usual time that she now knew precisely to be six in the morning. She slipped her feet into her sandals and pulled a clean white shift over her head. She didn't know if she was tired or refreshed. For the past three nights since their return from Tortola, increasingly she was feeling as if she were living two lives, the one right now with her feet on the floor and sunlight just beginning to come through the windows. And the other one, the one of her dreams. But were they dreams? As she thought back to last night, her memories were as real to her as where she was standing right now. She should be exhausted, but she wasn't. She should be afraid, but she wasn't. She would wait for whoever was coming for her and she would surrender herself. In the meantime, there were goats to milk and cheese to make.

But they didn't come. The day turned into another day, then two and three. There were no signs of the men Nita knew were chasing her. She began to relax, at least a bit. Jorge and Pepe returned to their foraging at the dump; Nita tended to her goats. She also spent increasing time with Carmine, teaching her the details of cheese making. The trick, she shared was nothing special, just keeping everything incredibly clean and all the milk and whey uncontaminated. The mastery was in the attention to detail.

After a week without a sign of threat, Jorge and Pepe begged Nita to go with them to the Friday night open air vids in the parking lot in the Valley. There was a vid playing about a group of super spies, jacked of course. Perhaps Nita could learn a bit about how to use her tech.

At first Nita resisted. But then she thought about the cheese tarts and berry flavored yogurt drinks she could sell to the movie goers. The trips back and forth from Tortola had depleted her savings and it would be good to make a few pounds. Working with Carmine she began making her preparations to have plenty to sell - and hopefully to sell out before the vid started so that she would not miss any of it

*****

Mike and another sunburned tourist wearing a vintage Hawaiian shirt stood in front of the steel shuttered store front of what had once been Ernesto's nameless tech shop. They worked hard at making a big deal of looking through digital maps and listening to tour guide audios as they pointed in multiple directions. The tech they carried and wore spoke to money to burn.

At the bottom of the alley, fifty feet away, a second group of six decidedly less affluent looking men loitered, smoking cigarettes and occasionally eying the two tourists. Anyone passing by would assume that they were casing the tourists for a quick mark.

Over the drone of the tour guide's digital voice, Bill leaned over and whispered in Mike's ear, "It's completely shielded. Whatever's behind there is electromagnetically masked."

Mike nodded and pointed in a different direction than Bill was looking in and then started walking down the alley in the direction of the men standing at the corner.

"Yeah," Mike said. "Kinda figured. Knew it had to be too good to be true." Along with Bill, he walked past the six men, pointedly ignoring their stares, and doing everything he could not to laugh.

"So where to now?" Bill said in a loud voice, looking around.

"I'm beat," Mike replied in an equally loud voice. "Let's go back to the boat."

Given the agency's impressive capture rate for contraband runners, Mike and Bill along with their three-man crew had more than enough sea-faring yachts to choose from for their trip to the Caribbean. The 'boat' was a Hanse 1595, circa 2052, borrowed from the NAA-BI confiscated property yard. Two days after selecting the boat, it was hard to recognize its original interior of teak and leather hidden behind the tech that was squeezed into every possible spare space.

Taking on the personas of wealthy robber barons out for a good time made sense. It allowed Mike and Bill to roam around with tech of all shapes and sizes draped clumsily around their body and hard-jacked to their own sprockets with micro thin blue wires. The important stuff of course was what was inside their heads and torsos.

The six additional members of the team had been in place already for several years in the Caribbean as part of the NAA's ongoing infiltration of the contraband business. Over the past forty-eight hours they had been polling their resources looking for any signs of exotic tech.

As expected, the active signal from Julia's tech had gone silent after a few hours. Unexpectedly, and intensely disappointedly, however, it had not come back online since then. Mike had hoped that the signal would return as whoever was using her tech tried to gain access to the secrets it held. But there had only been silence since then.

All they had to go on now was the low frequency ping that the passive chip emitted. At best, the range for the signal was five miles. It had to be that way to avoid draining the power required to keep the chip operative. Theoretically, in its inactive state, with occasional bursts of active transmission, the chip could operate indefinitely drawing on the natural electromagnetic pulses of the human body. That was why the chip was still operative more than six months after Julia had gone dark.

Mike and Bill had driven every inch of Tortola at least three times, playing their part as lost tourists, searching for the telltale ping. Nothing. Their six-man team on the ground had done the same. And with the same results. Their only lead had been rumors of this shop on a nameless alley and someone called 'Ernie' who was its proprietor.

Back on the boat they disgustedly threw their pouches and bags on the sole table without anything on it.

"Damn," Bill said. "So, what the hell do we do now?"

"Beats me," Mike responded, sitting down in a chair next to the table. "I guess we'll have to tell the ground crew to keep on digging and see if they can find anything."

"Damn, you know I hate doing that. The longer we keep this up, it jeopardizes the agency's long-term goals." Bill opened the small fridge and pulled out two bottles of filtered water and placed them on the table.

"Yeah, but if we don't, we're totally dead in the water. We've got nothing." As Mike spoke, the boat swayed, and the two bottles of water slid across the table as both men reached out quickly to catch them. They laughed, but in the end Mike finally decided to soft-jack a message to Roberto, their team lead on the island.

> *Any news? Out of ideas here. Hard-jack 13:00 tomorrow.*

* * * * *

In the 2030s, when sprocket technology was moving from fantasy to fact, most researchers and developers at Dr Raymond Mallards' think tank were exploring thought recognition as the operational foundation. And were failing miserably. It wasn't the tech that was the problem, it was the organic component that was revealing limitations. Apart from a few Zen masters and Tibetan yogis, the human subjects simply did not have clean enough thought patterns to make thought-only interfaces effective and reliable. Some of the test results were humorous; some were tragic. All failed.

The alternative was to develop two interfaces. The first, soon to be called, soft jacking, consisted of a heads-up visual overlay that could be manipulated through a wide variety of single-word or short phase commands expressed by sub vocalizations, blink sequences, shoulder twitches, and finger shadowing.

This method allowed Mike to send his short message to his team lead, Roberto, while sitting in the cabin drinking a bottle of water. Roberto would receive the message as a recurring ping in his inner ear until he accessed his own heads-up display and through a rapid double eye blink opened and responded to the message.

Their longer conversation would require the second option. One, or both of them, would be hard-jacked. That could be to a display if they wanted to share with friends, or a G-watch, G-chip, G-cube, or some other similar gadget for a more private conversation.

So, at 13:00 the next day, Mike and Bill both connected blue filament cables from their wrist sprockets to a one-inch square cube of the same blue color sitting on the table between them. Ten minutes later, Roberto's voice echoed in both of their heads.

> *Guys, we gotta stop doing this,* Roberto's voice reverberated in Mike and Bill's heads.
>
> *Sorry,* Mike subvocalized. *But we're stuck. Any news?*
>
> *Yeah, quite a bit actually so I'll make this real quick. Too many bodies around. Turns out that shop you were looking at is, or rather was, operated by one of King Chronos's princes. A guy by the name of Ernesto Smith.*
>
> *Anyway, word is that King Chronos, himself, wants the tech. He's got a goon squad out looking for the girl.*

Girl? That was news to Mike. Well at least the search was down to half of the population.

> *Yeah, that's the other thing we found out. Some kids on Virgin Gorda found a body on the beach, Julia I guess, and extracted the tech. Then they went to Ernesto's and of all things, he installed the tech in the girl. I'm told that she's a half-Asian looker. Rest of story is confusing. But it seems that she escaped with these two young boys with some tech. Search*

is moving to Virgin Gorda. Recommend you head there too.

Listen, gotta go. Guests.

The connection dropped. Mike and Bill stared at each other. They had a lead.

* * * * *

Ernie winced. The words sounded like thunder in his head. How was the King able to do that? *Get the tech! We've got NAA-BI crawling around now in addition to the NAA agents we already know about! Two ridiculous agents posing as tourists, sun burned, flower shirts. Take them out too!*

Ernie winced again. NAA-BI just like the heads-up on the screen? Oh shit! This was getting out of hand. *Look, Sire,* he subvocalized, trying to sound as if he wasn't pleading. *We think they may have gone to Virgin Gorda.*

So, what the frack are you doing talking to me!?! Find her! Kill them! Ernie's eyes watered, and he reflexively brought his hands up to cover his ears. He had to find out how the King was doing this. But at least he already had his men on Virgin Gorda. How hard could it be to find a girl on an island that size?

* * * * *

Nita and Carmine finished packing the last of the jugs of yogurt-fruit drinks into the cooler. Jorge and Pepe each grabbed an end and carried the heavy box outside and tied it down in the cart attached to one of the bikes.

Nina was happy that Carmine had agreed to join them at the vids tonight. She had come to value the companionship of another female. While she loved her brothers very much, they were, after all, boys. She could talk girl stuff with Carmine. And most importantly, Carmine's laughter distracted her from the unrelenting din of voices filling her head.

The four bikes, two with carts trailing behind them, made their way on the eight-mile trip along the coastal road to the Valley. Nita had insisted that they leave early so that they could be sure to get a table in the market strategically placed for the most foot traffic. She knew that she would easily sell everything tonight, but she wanted to make sure that she did so quickly so that she and Carmine could join the boys for the entire vid. Jorge and Pepe would also be able to lay out a flanket close to the front for all four of them.

Their timing was perfect. Nita grabbed a table a third of the way down the path that all the vid-goers were taking to the parking lot where the screen was set up. She and Carmine set their cheese platters and a sample of yogurt drinks on a crisp white linen table cloth and waited. As expected, business was brisk. Vid-goers lined up impatiently with their mugs, thermoses, and glasses to have the cool yogurt drinks poured into their open containers.

The flow of customers screeched to a halt when one of the two sunburned tourists standing in front of her held up an empty hand. "Sorry, forgot to bring a thermos," he said in what Nita immediately recognized as an NAA accent.

"We have two we can sell to you. Is that okay?" Nita asked. *Tourist,* she thought. *Wasteful, thinking money could buy anything.*

Nita felt an uncomfortable sense of being watched as she reached into the bottom of the cooler for two battered thermoses that had been harvested from the dump by her brothers. One of the men was staring at her intently and especially at her wrists that she had wrapped in pretty bits of lace to hide the hideous scars and her sprockets. To make matters worse, her tech was on fire. There was a pinging inside her ear that wouldn't stop.

"Thanks, what's your name?" the blonde-haired tourist with the horrible sunburn asked.

"Nita," she said without thinking. But as soon as the words came out of her mouth, her sense of alarm was triggered. Did they know?

"Pretty name." he said and then, their new thermos filled with yogurt drinks, he and the other tourist walked away into the crowd.

A chill went up Nita's back even though it was still over 90 degrees as the sun was going down. The pinging inside her head stopped once the two men were out of sight. She dismissed the sense of foreboding she felt and turned to help Carmine hand out the last of their yogurt and cheese to the vid-goers and then quickly wrap up their wares and store everything in one of the coolers. They each grabbed an end and made their way to the parking lot where the sound of the vids already filled the air.

* * * * *

We found her! We found Julia! Mike soft-jacked to Bill.

"Damn, this stuff is really good," Bill said out loud as he drank from the bent lip of the thermos.

Positioning team, Mike continued, looking around for the rest of the men. He had taken the forethought to relocate the Tortola team to Virgin Gorda the previous evening and could now see the six men paired off, scattered throughout the crowd. Even two of the crew members from the yacht were here standing at the back of the parking lot.

West Indian-Asian mix. Looker. Mike caught sight of Nita and the other girl moving through the seated crowd toward the front of the lot closest to the screen. *Up front.*

Got it! Shut up! Mike looked around wondering where Roberto was soft-jacking from. He caught sight of him with one of the other team members maneuvering to buy a beer at one of the booths still open on the path out of the parking lot.

Good plan, Mike thought as he realized that Roberto was positioning himself to block the exit.

The crowd of over 100 people, some resting on flankets or ordinary blankets, and some sitting in chairs at the back, quieted down as the main feature began. Mike and Bill, having neither, stood at the back of the parking lot along with a crowd of fifty or so other onlookers. Including, Mike noticed, not sure if he should be relieved or worried, a dozen or so police uniforms.

Scanning the crowd, he also noticed that everyone else standing in the back was doing exactly the same thing. It was a game, he realized. The pickpockets, thieves, and general trouble makers watching their marks in the distracted crowd of vid-goers. And the police watching the predators.

Three men in particular, caught Mike's attention as he watched them pointing in Nita's direction. One of them looked up and in Mike and Bill's direction. *Shit!* Mike knew they were made.

As he watched, one of the men split off from the three and began moving around the back of the crowd in their direction, Mike had an idea. He tapped Bill on the arm and then pointed to a group of four policemen. He quickly took his g-watch off and pocketed it. Then, making a show of what he was doing, he walked over to the closest group of policemen and began protesting in a loud voice. "Officers, over there," he pointed. "Those are the men who stole my g-watch. See!" He held up his left wrist with the visible white, un-sunburned band of skin where the watch had just been.

His protests had the desired effect as the man circling behind them stopped in his tracks and began to turn away. Mike pointed in his direction. "That's him! That's the man!"

People in the crowd began turning around protesting about all the noise. And then everything went south. Mike saw out of the corner of his eye the two other men, taking advantage of the distraction, stepping through the crowd in Nita's direction. Helplessly, he watched, letting Bill do the explaining to the police about the theft, as Nita was being dragged away.

And then it got interesting again. Roberto, along with a group of vid-goers were now surrounding Nita and the two men, blocking them from leaving the parking lot. Vid-goers all around the area, very familiar with Nita and her small cheese business, began shouting and calling for the pols.

Mike added his own voice to the fray. "Officers, look over there! Someone is trying to kidnap that poor girl!"

Chaos continued as more male vid-goers stepped in and began pummeling the would-be kidnappers. The police, having two crimes to manage, split up with the majority going to the aid of Nita while two captured the third man accused of the theft.

It only took a few minutes before the would-be thief and two pols were standing in front of Mike. "Is this the guy?" one of them asked shoving a complaining man roughly in front of them. Delight was evident on their faces at the ease of their catch. It wasn't often that they could be so successful in helping out the quasi tourists. Rewards would be forthcoming.

Mike, even though he was an analyst, had still learned a few tricks of the trade. In the middle of the confusion he was able to slip his g-watch from his pocket and drop it at the feet of the accused thief.

"There it is! That's my g-watch!" he pointed at the watch lying in the dirt at the feet of the man. "I know it because of the custom bezel," he explained. He reached down and quickly picked it up and shook it in the face of the totally confused man being held between the two policemen.

"What the frack are you talking about?" the man screamed, bewildered by the sudden turn of events.

Somewhere in the middle of the melee the vid had been turned off, no doubt to protect the equipment from any incidental damage. Mike found himself conducting two conversations at the same time. Yes, it was his watch, and this was the man who had taken it from his wrist at the market. And yes, he wanted to press charges.

At the same time, he could see the other, larger, group of police rounding up the two other men. But where was Nita? Just then he heard Roberto's voice soft jacked into his head. *Girl safe. Taking home. Will guard.*

Mike relaxed, even though he was still shaking with adrenalin. Knowing that Nita was safe for at least awhile, he focused his attention on the capture of the three men and putting them out of action. Two hours later, he left the police station with assurances that the men would spend at least the next forty-eight hours behind reinforced smart glass. He loved when a plan worked out.

* * * * *

Nita woke up. Or at least she thought she did. She wasn't sure anymore. Was last night a dream or was this time in the dark waiting for the sun to come up the dream? Memories came flooding in - being grabbed from behind and yanked to her feet … the rush of other arms pulling her away … the fight … the pols. Then, the strangest of all, the man with the bad teeth and foul breath whispering in her ear that she was safe and being taken care of. Just wait.

She remembered the pols driving her home, asking questions, probing but polite, assuming she was just another pretty girl that someone wanted to grab. And then Jorge, Pepe and Carmine coming behind at a slower pace, pulling her bike with them. And then even later, after the pols had left, listening as they described the men who shared the same message with them. Nita was safe and being guarded.

And yet, in the midst of it all, there were still goats to milk and chickens to feed. That, she knew was real. Getting dressed quickly, she walked into the kitchen and caught sight of cups, plates, knives, and forks scattered about from last night. So, that really was real too, all of it.

The sun was up by the time she had cleaned the kitchen, attended to the shrines and made herself a cup of coffee. She walked outside, enjoying the cool breeze that would remain for the next hour or so until the sweltering heat set in.

Just as she was opening the chicken coop fence, she picked up on the hum of an electric car on the road below. Then the sound stopped and was replaced by the sound of an opening and closing car door. She hesitated, then continued to walk into the chicken coop and check for eggs. Whatever was going to happen, was going to happen. She was too exhausted to resist.

The chickens were generous this morning. Nita walked out of the chicken coop with a basket of ten eggs … and almost bumped into a man who she immediately recognized from last night. She gasped.

"Sorry to frighten you," the man exclaimed and took the basket from her hands. "Guess, you've been frightened a lot these days."

He was one of the sunburned men without a thermos from last night. She looked past him and could see Jorge in the door of the house with a cricket bat in his hands and relaxed just a bit.

"What do you want?" she asked. "Who are you?"

"I'm a friend. I helped you last night. I want to talk." Mike explained. his voice surprised Nita in its softness. "Is that coffee I smell?" he asked. For a moment, his eyes lost their focus, then he was back to looking at her with a smile. "Oh, and can you ask your brother to put down that bat thing?"

She sighed and made a motion with her hand to Jorge. "I can't do this anymore. Come on, I guess there's eggs enough for everyone this morning."

You are so much like her." Mike murmured under his breath as he followed her into the house.

* * * * *

The eggs were good. Mike did everything but lick the plate. Scrambled with goat cheese, sun dried tomatoes and a few fresh herbs they were better than anything he'd had in years. But not the coffee - which was decidedly not coffee at all. Only the cream from the goats saved it.

The pretty girl refused to talk about anything serious while they ate, insisting that digestion required calmness. Instead, they discussed improved egg production and whether they should move the goat herd to the public grazing lands a few miles away.

It was only when the plates were put away, that the conversation turned to Mike's reason for being there.

"I'm here to help you," Mike explained. "The tech that you've got, that you found on the beach, belonged to a phenomenal NAA-BI agent by the name of Julia. A real hero." He couldn't hide the sadness he felt as he explained the work that Julia did for the agency and the goodness of her heart.

"You've probably figured it out, but It's very, very, special tech. Secret, research stuff, actually." Mike paused, uncertain of how much to be sharing with these three individuals, barely more than children.

But then he realized how much he was going to need their help and trust over the weeks, and maybe even years to come. Trust started with his ability to be open with them.

"Look," he explained. "I was her handler, the guy who designed the tech, taught her how to use it." He paused and looked at Nita with concern on his face. "I honestly don't know how you're surviving right now. It took Julia years to learn how to use that tech."

"You want me to go with you so that you can teach me how to use it and be like Julia." Nita's voice was calm and steady as she finished Mike's message for him. *Julia, so that was the name of the voice in her head.* "That's why you're here. To take me away."

The look on Mike's face expressed both gratitude and surprise at her comprehension. "Yes, and we need to leave quickly before King Chronos sends another team to grab you. We've found out that he's aware of the uniqueness of your tech and wants it badly for his own. Its literally a matter of national security ..." Mike's voice dropped off as he saw the looks of disgust on the three faces in front of him.

"Anyway ..." he stammered, trying to get back into their good graces. "We really do need to go. He's a bad guy and will do bad things to you if he catches you."

Nina leaned back in her chair and folded her arms across her chest. "So ... I have a choice between being your prisoner or his."

Mike squirmed. He desperately wanted them to come with him voluntarily. But in essence she was right. "I'm nicer?" he asked, looking into each of their faces in turn.

Nita picked up on Mike's glances at the others around the table. "And what about them? Do they come too?"

"It's up to them." Mike explained. "My instructions are only for you. But I'm sure that I can make accommodations for everyone."

Pepe's eyes got huge across the table. "NAA? Nita, please ..."

Jorge, too, was wide-eyed with excitement. He vigorously nodded his agreement.

It was only Carmine who shook her head negatively. Which was a good thing. Someone had to care for the chickens and goats.

* * * * *

"Just one more thing," Nita said after the kitchen was cleaned up and the last goodbyes with Carmine were made, including handing her the keys and the secret recipes for all of Nita's creations. She walked over to the family shrine and took a small conch shell, a pipe and a set of beads from the table. It would have to do as tokens of her mother and their shared beliefs. As an afterthought, she lifted a stone tablet below the shrine and reached into a hollow area to pull their papers out. With her back to Mike, she stuffed their papers into her shoulder bag along with the few articles from the shrine.

As they were walking out the door, most likely for the last time, another thought occurred to her. Nita touched Mike's arm and asked, "Would you like to see where we buried Julia?"

Mike turned and faced her with a stunned look on his face. "You buried her? Where?"

"Up there." Nita pointed up the steep path that the goats took to the higher grazing areas. "It will only take a minute."

She led him then, followed by her brothers, to the place where they had buried her and covered the grave with a cairn of island stones. Over the past months, Nita had planted Columbias and Plumeria around the spot and their vibrant colors led to a sense of peacefulness.

As they stood looking down on the grave, Mike remained silent. Nita could see the moistness around his eyes. After a moment he reached into the small touristy pack strapped around his waist and pulled out a small silver disc. He leaned down over the grave and placed it under one of the rocks. He paused a moment with his head dropped down and then slowly got up and turned to all three of them. "Thank you – but now we really need to go."

* * * * *

They left with only the clothes on their backs and Nita's shoulder bag. Nina hugged Carmine one last time and joined Mike, Jorge and Pepe to walk down the side of the hill to where Mike's car was parked. "Do you have a helo?" she asked Mike.

"No, why?"

"Because there's one coming in across the channel from Tortola."

Awareness dawned for Mike. They had waited too long and now they were in trouble again. "Move it, everyone!" he half slid-ran down the side of the hill towards the car. At the bottom he opened the door and motioned all three of them to crowd into the back seat. "Under the tarp." He explained. "It will block your heat signatures."

As he came around to the side of the car and got in, he at last could hear the whup-whup of the helo coming in their direction. He paused for a moment and then punched the ignition button. There was no way that they were going to outrun even a bicycle in this tiny solar car, especially given the three passengers hidden in the back. Deception was required. He opened all the windows and pulled the car away at a leisurely, touristy pace.

"By the way," he explained in a voice barely more than a whisper, looking straight ahead out the windshield of the car. "Roberto is taking care of Carmine right now. I hope he doesn't scare her too much. He's pretty rough looking." He smiled to himself at the thought of Roberto with his wild hair and broken teeth trying to convince pretty little Carmine that he was there to help her. He desperately hoped that she let him help her. Otherwise …

"I'll keep quiet after this, but when we get to the pier, you'll see two men waiting next to a sea-green skimmer. Run for it and jump in. I'll catch up as best as I can later." The sound of the helo was louder. Mike hoped that it was heading for the house they had just left and hadn't noticed the tourist driving casually towards Spanish Town and the pier.

Their luck held, and they arrived at the abandoned ferry pier without incident. The sound of the helo had stopped about five minutes ago which meant that whoever was onboard was now on the ground and looking for Nita. Mike shuddered at the thought of what might happen if they caught Carmine and Roberto.

Under his breath he hissed, "Out," as he opened the back side door while the car was still in motion. "Just jump in the skimmer. Quick."

First Jorge and Pepe, and then finally Nita, rolled out of the door onto the asphalt and then got to their feet to cover the last few feet to the small boat. In coordination with their efforts, the two men standing casually beside the boat threw a tarp over them and pushed the boat into the tide. In a minute they were pulling away headed toward another Hanse 1595 similar to the one that Mike and Bill had arrived on.

Mike, with barely a pause, continued driving around the parking lot, making a show of finding a convenient parking spot. He resisted the urge to smile as he figuratively patted himself on the back for his superior plan. At last, after a good five minutes he pulled into a spot, got out and stretched. Then he took the short walk to the main street and entered a gaudy-looking bar typically frequented by both locals and tourists. With a smile, he greeted his partner Bill who was already seated at the bar drinking something that looked fruity and frothy.

They spent the next half hour conducting two separate conversations as they downed a significant number of the ridiculous drinks with umbrellas in them. "Man, there's nothing to do in this damn place." Mike complained loudly to Bill. "After you've seen the Baths, what else is there? Just look at this place," he dramatically, in his best drunken stupor, swiveled in his chair and looked out at the early morning crowd of patrons. "What a bunch of deadbeats."

Angry stares of patrons greeted him but then quickly dismissed his ramblings as those of just another drunken tourist, no doubt protected by one of the profiteers in the harbor. A voice from a dark corner recklessly offered a suggestion. "Then maybe you should leave and go somewhere else – like the Florida swamps."

Mike turned back to the bar to finish his drink and nodded at his partner. "Bill, I do believe he has a point there."

While they were playing out this drama, another conversation was going on through their sprockets.

> Mike: *They're on their way to the Julia Too*
> Bill: *Good, Chronos bought off the pols… now surrounding the Julia One*
> Mike: *Julia Too soon to be leaving channel and into Atlantic. Need to distract*

They again nodded wordlessly to each other and dropped from their bar stools to clumsily make their way through the tables toward the door.

Applauding their departure, the same voice echoed from the back of the bar. "And good riddance."

Both Mike and Bill returned the favor by flipping the universal salute over their departing shoulders.

Once outside in the sweltering heat of late morning, their pace and gait became more intentional.

"My God, but those things tasted terrible. My mouth is stuck closed with syrup." Bill complained as he made a face, trying to swish saliva around to clear out his mouth.

"Focus," Mike said, as he walked with Bill to where their own skimmer was tied at the end of the last pier. "This part could get tricky."

A man in dress whites was standing at attention and saluted them as they approached. "Mr. Barnes and Mr. Noble," he said in a crisp voice. "Are you ready to return to the Julia One?"

"Right oh," Mike said, still playing the part of a drunken tourist. "Let's get off this frackin' island." He stepped into the skimmer making a show of partially losing his balance and letting the other man catch his fall.

"Mr. Barnes, careful there, " the man chided and led Mike to a seat in the middle of the boat. Mike was about to remind his that he was Nobles and that Bill was Barnes but decided to skip it. Instead, he watched as Bill staggered into the boat and found a seat next to him.

They pushed off and quickly they were beyond the shallow waves of the harbor and headed to the Julia One.

Mike expressed an inner sigh of relief when he saw the circle of small Pols boats surrounding the Julia One and the absence of the Julia Too that until just recently had been anchored at the edges of the harbor. Now all they had to do was to delay as much as they could.

Once on deck, they were greeted by the same pols captain who had worked with them the previous evening to incarcerate the three thieves – who were now standing on either side of him.

"Well, well, Mr's Noble and Barnes," the captain said, nervously shifting his eyes to the left and right without moving his head. "We seem to have a small misunderstanding that needs to be cleared up." He cleared his throat and continued. "It has come to my attention that the story you told us last night might not be completely accurate."

Mike did his best to draw himself up into the posture of a drunk trying to be serious. "Why are you on our boat?" he asked belligerently. "We want to leave this godforsaken island immediately!" he shouted. "Malcolm," he yelled in his most stringent voice towards the two men who were crewing the boat for him and were standing near the stern. "Let's go home."

Suddenly there were two guns pointed at Mike and Bill, respectively. "Not quite yet." The captain said in an even more nervous voice. "Not until we search this ship. You are under suspicion of kidnapping."

Mike took a half-step back, now genuinely nervous. They may not find Nita on board but there was enough tech in the main cabin to cause unlimited problems and suspicions, not least of which was having it removed and undoubtedly in the hands of King Chronos. But then he caught the wink from one of the two crewmen and relaxed. "Go ahead, be my guests." he said.

* * * * *

Three hours later they were at last pulling up anchor. Mike and Bill each holding up a beer in salute, grinned broadly to the four pols boats that were ready to escort them through the Drake Channel and into international waters. As the two of them outwardly chattered, an inner conversation continued with the two crewmen who were busily preparing to navigate the ship.

Mike: *Saved our asses. Quick thinking.*
Crewman one: *It was close ... picked up the message on pols scan just in time*
Mike: *Where's the tech?*
Crewman one: *Glug, glug*

Mike felt faint. Even with the unlimited approval the director had given to the project, the cost was going to be staggering.

But he felt better when he opened his saved messages.

Julia Too: *Family secured. Baltimore Harbor ETA eight hours.*

The charade continued until at last they were a mile past the boundaries of the Caribbean Sea and the Atlanta that constituted the quasi-legal territory claims of the ICVI. With flourish, they at once raised the flag of the NAA and began searching for the Julia Too.

CHAPTER 5

NAA-BI headquarters, Washington-Baltimore corridor

"Now tell me again why you decided to commission a second ship from the yard?" The director asked, glaring at Mike who was seated across from him.

The look on the director's face was hard for Mike to assess. First, the praise had been effusive for bringing in Nita voluntarily, and most importantly, without any obvious damage to the tech. But as the story of the last few days began to unfold the details of the expenses, including tossing their own tech overboard and the now revealing the commission of the second yacht, the tone of the director's voice was decidedly changing.

"That was half of your budget for the next eighteen months. You do know that, don't you?" Director Walker's rant continued while Mike sat and patiently took his beating. He knew that the fact that they had found Nita and the tech far outweighed any other concerns. He just had to sit here and wait until his boss calmed down.

"Boss," Mike explained, "You said anything, do absolutely anything to get her back. As I recall, your words were 'you have an infinite budget'. I did what I had to do." Mike shrugged his shoulders as if to say, 'what can you do about it?'

"Alright," Director Walker sighed, indicating his surrender. "But you're going to help me explain this to our benefactor, and the story better be more convincing than the one you just told me." He paused, and then added. "And we better find out quick, why on earth, Julia was in the Virgin Islands and found, of all things, in a dump. It doesn't make any sense."

"Can I bring them in?" Mike asked. "They're really only kids and they are scared out of their wits."

Director Walker waved his hand in a disgusted motion of approval.

Mike got up and walked to the outer door. He took a deep sigh, opened it, and stepped into the outer office. Nita and her two brothers were sitting on the couch together in rapt attention to the vid screen that filled the entire wall opposite them. Jorge's and Pepe's eyes were so wide that they were in danger of leaping out of their heads. Nita, Mike noticed, was far more reserved, as if her mind was on something else, which it indeed probably was.

Nita nodded at Mike and then simultaneously tapped the knees of her two brothers sitting on either side of her. She stood up and dragged the boys with her who were decidedly resistant to pulling themselves away from whatever they were watching. After all, they had never seen holo projection, HOP, before.

Mike entered the inner office first and then began introductions as Nita and her brothers walked in uncertainly behind him. "Director Walker, I would like you to meet the Yamashita family, Juanita, Jorge and Pepe. Juanita, of course, is the individual with Julia's tech."

Mike motioned Nita to a chair directly in front of the Director and next to the chair he had just vacated. He led Jorge and Pepe to chairs on the side. The room suddenly felt very crowded.

Director Walker sat silently for a moment, staring at Nita. *You've got my tech, you goddamn bitch. I want it back. I'm getting it back.* The words remained unspoken as he choked them back. He hadn't gotten to where he was by speaking his inner thoughts.

Instead, he lifted his eyes and looked at each of the ensemble of individuals one at a time using his best peaceful but concerned expression. Finally, he cleared his throat and began. "Welcome to NAA-BI headquarters and our research facility. I hope your trip was uneventful ..."He paused with a staged chuckle in an attempt to build repour by acknowledging the idiocy of his words.

Nita turned to look at Mike. It didn't take sprockets for her to communicate her initial opinion of the director.

"Sorry, that didn't come out right." The Director quickly apologized. "I know you've been in a near-death situation escaping from King Chronos and his thugs getting here. Mike and I would personally like to thank you for your decision to be our guests."

"But we're not guests, are we." Nita's voice was calm and matter of fact. Her face was a mask of tranquility as she stared at the director, waiting for his response.

Mike watched the exchange. He knew that her tech was yet to be fully activated and given access to the AI. All Mike had shown her was how to access public information domains, the Sproc-Net, and an all-purpose messaging system. And yet ...

The director cleared his throat. "No, I regret to say that you are technically correct. Until we resolve the problem of the tech that you've stolen, you'll have to stay under our guidance."

"We found it in the dump. It was thrown away!" Jorge inserted himself into the conversation. "We didn't steal anything!"

Nita looked back over her shoulder at her brother. "It's okay, Jorge." she said. "I think we should find a way to work with them. What other choice do we have?"

She turned back then and spoke directly to the director. "We made a big mistake." She began. "Jorge and Pepe found that dead and rotting woman in the dump and I took the sprockets out of her body myself. Then we went to an illegal tech shop on Tortola and had the tech jacked into me. I now know that was wrong and a mistake. How do I give it back to you?"

Nita had begun her statement with a firm voice. But by the time that she got to the last two sentences she appeared to be in distress and pleading for help.

Both the director and Mike picked up on the desperation. Mike however recognized something else, something incongruent about her request. There were games going on within games. He leaned forward, opening his mouth to ask a question.

The director held up his hand to halt Mike as he was about to speak. "Juanita, I wish with my whole heart and soul that we could take it back from you. If it was any other normal tech, we could extract it or at least make it inoperable." He paused, observing her and recognizing the same patterns that he found in himself and he had seen in Julia. "But you know this, don't you, its too late. Its already integrating into your nervous system. It's already becoming part of you and … removing it would most certainly kill you."

"No!" Jorge jumped out of his chair, took three steps and reached across the desk toward Director Walker. "You're not going to kill my sister!"

Just in time, Mike reached out and grabbed Jorge by the waist-band and pulled him back. The director stared at Jorge in genuine shock from where he had pushed back his chair against the HOP behind him which was still rippling as it bent to absorb his weight.

"Jorge, calm down. No one's going to kill your sister." Mike pleaded even as he took a quick look at the director to make sure he wasn't lying.

"No, Jorge, we're not going to kill her, or either of you for that matter. But …" The director pulled his chair back up to the desk, straightened the pleated silk ruffle at his neck and cleared his throat again. "You do have a choice …. If you choose not to cooperate with us in regard to helping us work with this tech, then that's fine."

Even though the director's words said one thing, his eyes told a different story as he looked back and forth between Mike and Nita.

He continued, ignoring the glare from Mike and the zen-like calm but piercing stare from Nita. "We'll find a place to house you where all of you can be quite comfortable as long as necessary."

The director sat forward and put his elbows on the desk, taking ownership of the space. "Juanita," he said, "we would very much like you to work with us. The tech you are now in possession of is very valuable and frankly the very fact that it is working within you is testimonial to excellent chances that you can be useful to our cause."

In the midst of the tension around her, Nita remained motion-less. "What is your cause?" she asked in a voice barely above a whisper.

"I'll let Dr Carson, Mike to you, gather some people for the explanation. We'll give you time to make your decision, however long it takes. But I truly believe that once you listen to what we have to say, you will consider it an honor to work with us. And ..." the director turned his attention to Jorge and Pepe. "I assure you that we can offer a future to your brothers here, in our on-campus school, that they could find nowhere else."

* * * * *

There wasn't anything else to say after that. Mike ushered Nita and her brothers out the door. Director Walker waited until he heard the outer office door open and close and then pressed his thumbs to each of the corners of the desk. A virtual screen slid up in the middle of the stack of papers in front of him. Within a few seconds a grey-haired head turned around and smiled at him.

"Frank, what a pleasure. Please tell me that we have good news."

"Yes, sir, we might. I just met with the girl. She's clearly feeling the neurological effects of the implants. It's definitely digging into her cortex and hippocampus just as it's supposed to. I think she might be willing to cooperate as well. We won't have to coerce her."

"Oh good. I'm so happy to hear that. We've had so many failures in the past that truly break my heart. When we lost precious Julia, I thought that it might be the end. I simply don't know how I'm going to break the news to her parents and siblings."

"I understand, sir. We'll do our best to make up for the loss."

The connection dropped, but the virtual display remained in place. Within a minute another well-preserved face appeared. Director Walker forced his voice to remain calm even though the steely stare facing him sent chills up his back. "Madam secretary, please pardon the interruption. But I felt it important to share what I hope is good news."

"Frank, I'm rather busy at the moment. But make it quick." Her eyes swiveled to left and right indicating to Frank that she was not alone and to be discreet.

"Yes, mam, We found that package that went missing, You now the one with the great wrapper. Well we found the contents but in different packaging, but apparently undamaged."

The secretary's eyes opened wide for a moment then quickly settled back into her normative frown. She coughed. "Oh, my Frank, that is good news, but so strange. Let me clear my schedule and come out to see you. Would tomorrow be okay? I'd love to see the new wrapping and of course check the contents."

Director Walker was about to nod in agreement when the screen went blank and slid back into the desk. For a moment he sat looking blankly across the room and then, raising his eyebrows and shaking his head, he returned to the work in front of him. The action lists were long and there was much work to be done, especially now that Julia was gone.

CHAPTER 6

Nita ran her hands over the velvety texture of the arms of the chair. At least that's what she now believed that velvet felt like. It felt similar to, but even softer and smoother than the couch in Ernie's workshop. Twice in two weeks? This was such a strange world she had entered.

Even the chair itself was new to her. Chairs were hard and inflexible and had straight backs or were made of webbing slung between metal poles. This one, however, was like a massive sea sponge with huge arms that wrapped around her and cushions softer than any bed she had ever experienced.

She let herself sink back as she struggled to organize her thinking. It was becoming increasingly complex as each day passed. It was not that she had trouble reasoning through whatever was on her mind. It was just that it felt like there were two or three people inside her, each competing for dominance. When she could focus on thinking, her mind was crisper than she could ever remember. But increasingly, there were the other voices demanding equal time. It wasn't actually voices … more a disconnected, incomplete, cloud of images, memories not her own, insights not based on her experience, thoughts that she felt were important but didn't know why, ... Sometimes when she walked down the halls with her perennial escorts or was in this part of the building, the voices shouted out to her in particular intensity, almost as if someone was calling out to her. it went on and on, waking and sleeping. Nothing fell into order. She was exhausted and exnihilated at the same time. She wanted it to stop.

"Nita, are you okay?"

A hand shook Nita's arm. She opened her eyes and saw Mike standing over her with a look of concern on his face. As she looked around, she saw several other faces, seven her mind told her without counting, some familiar such as the other agent called Bill, but others as well who she had never seen before or perhaps only in passing. Even so, there was a familiarity about them.

Nita pushed herself up as best she could in the ridiculous chair. "Just thinking," she mumbled and rubbed her eyes. She wanted badly to scratch her sprockets which over the last two days had increasingly started to itch and burn. Unfortunately, the jar of calendula salve which would give her relief was sitting on the small table in her bedroom a very long way away.

"We're ready to begin." Mike explained and then sat down in a chair similar to Nita's on her left side and looked at her one more time with concern.

"Alright then," he began. "Everyone, this is Juanita. She prefers to be called Nita." He paused and quickly glanced at Nita again. "We're here to give Nita some background about who Julia was and what we do here at the agency. Let's begin by making short introductions so she'll know who her team is. Then we can proceed to provide her with the information she needs so she can figure out how she wants to work with us."

Seated in an uneven circle around the room, men and women each took turns then to provide Nita with a name and a description of the role they had played in Julia's life and anticipated playing in her life. She noticed how they looked at her, some with curiosity, some with caution and others with unveiled suspicion. When they were finished, she also realized that she could recite their names, one after another, without missing a single one. She also sensed which had been friends and which were not.

"Alright then," Mike said. "Nita, I really couldn't describe what we do here better than the way that our benefactor, Dr. Raymond Mallard, did when he first conceived of the mission for our organization." As he was talking, he reached into a pocket on the side of his leg to pull out a small translucent pad and touch it a few times.

Nita jumped up in her seat, startled by the figure that suddenly shimmered in the open space in front of them. Embarrassed, she quickly shrank back into the chair cushions and then just as quickly leaned forward in anticipation. This of course was a holo. Something totally ordinary for all of these strange people but something new and marvelous to her.

A small smile crossed Mike's face as he noticed Nita's surprise. But he said nothing. He touched his pad and the holo started to move.

A tan skinned man with silver grey hair paced back and forth in front of them and then stopped directly in front of Nita. Unconsciously she dug her fingers into the arms of the chair.

"We're got a problem. And of course, we all know that. And we all know that its getting worse. A few of us are old enough to remember a time when we could walk down the street of an urban city and not have the possibility in our minds that a bomb might go off or a truck might come careening around a corner at us. There was a time when an attack on civilians would make the evening news and we would feel shock and horror rather than the indifference we feel now.

The efforts by various organizations, countries and even individuals to tear apart the fabric of civilization for their own benefit has become appallingly effective. Increasingly, we are no longer an open society moving freely about. For those of us who can afford it, we have drawn ourselves into enclaves, corporate parks, institutional gardens ... all the names we give to walled communities bent on protecting what is ours and damn with anything or anyone else. For everyone else who no longer has the safety net of reliable infrastructure ... water, sewer, electric, trash pickup, well....

The silver-haired man paused and stared directly at Nita who pulled herself back in her chair. His intense blue eyes seemed to look right through her.

Even as the enemy and the nature of warfare has fundamentally changed, we have continued to use our obsolete methods of reactive investigation after the fact. And we are failing miserably. We need a different approach. Indeed, that is what I want to propose today ... a different approach to countering the erosion of our society.

The silver-haired man started to pace and appeared to be speaking to someone out of sight of the holo. And then he turned once again toward Nita and continued.

Terrorism came to this country and thrived because of the incredible and unforeseen ability, supported by our new communication infrastructures, of those on the margins to find each other. The disaffected and often disturbed of our own culture who we shamefully neglected to care for, suddenly had the ability to find others of like minds halfway around the world. And those individuals, cults, and organizations who saw personal and communal benefit in tearing apart the fabric of western culture suddenly had the means to exploit these individuals and groups for their own gain. It just gets worse with every passing year. The ability of thugs like King Chronos, less than 100 miles off our coast, to effectively take over an entire population and create a new country in the Caribbean is just one example of what is happening around us.

The silver-haired man paused, put his hands in his pockets and looked at his feet. Then he looked up again directly at Nita.

In spite of this depressing picture that I have painted, I remain totally optimistic about the future of mankind. We are fundamentally good. But we've got to get a hell of a lot smarter.

First, we need to make better and different use of the technology around us. I've made no secret of the fact that since I invented and patented the Sprockets interfaces, that I've been working on an AI far more sophisticated than those in production today, one based on rosehip neuron infrastructure just like the sprockets technology.

Sprockets! Nita suddenly recognized this man. This was the famous inventor of the sprockets tech. He was said to be the richest man on the planet, indeed, in the solar system. Everyone said that he had become a recluse and hadn't been seen in public for decades.

To get to the point, since I do seem to ramble on a bit and perhaps my late wife was correct when she insisted that I missed my calling as a preacher ...

The holo paused for a moment looking down at the floor, then looked up again directly at Nita.

Anyway … I'm offering my AI to the North American Alliance to form a separate division, funded generously by me of course, to fix what's gone horribly wrong in the world.

Let me explain. First, we've been using AIs for decades to build algorithms to trace those individuals and organizations that are engaging in terrorism and other disruptions for their own benefit. We've gotten pretty good – to a point. But what we haven't been able to do is anticipate early enough where to interrupt the process. And no … I'm not talking about that old vid from the previous century about arresting people who will probably commit a crime. No, I mean something far more subtle than that. I mean interventions. Acts of kindness. But that's old stuff. I just propose that my AI, named Ruby, by the way, can do a much, much better job of it than anything you've got in place right now.

Now, here's the new stuff. Why can't we use the same approach that we use to track down everything that is wrong in our world, to begin to track down and support everything that could be good in our world? I know that we've always been limited by resources. Shoot, I know that every cent that gets collected in diminished taxes are spent in shoring up roads, the electric grid, water systems and everything else that has been systematically torn apart by terrorists. Public schools, social services are just part of my distant memory.

The bottom line, in the state that we are in, we can't help everyone all at once. But what if we knew the few who are most important to help first? What if we could anticipate and predict who, if given the right opportunity, could make a positive difference, could exponentially return on our investments.? What if we could make sure that these individuals and groups got all the support that they need to be optimally effective. And then, maybe we can help everyone. My AI can do that. And it can do that on a massive scale that hasn't been seen before. And, if you want it, it's yours.

Mike touched the pad in his hand and the holo froze in front of Nita.

"That was ten years ago," Mike explained. "And the people seated around you are that division."

Mike shut down the holo to give Nita a chance to look again at the faces in the room. She noticed some smiles directed at her but also still some suspicious frowns as well.

Mike touched his pad again and a second, and older but still handsome, image of Dr Mallard stood in front of Nita.

"This is from three years ago," Mike explained. It will help you to understand about Julia and about the tech that you have and how we got started working together." He paused to take a longer look at Nita. "Are you okay?" he asked softly as he leaned over and touched her arm resting on the chair arm. "You look flushed."

Nita pulled her arm back into her lap. She didn't want Mike to see the redness and swelling that was increasing in intensity around each of her sprockets. She felt that she was burning up but didn't want to interrupt what was happening right now. This was the information, even though she didn't understand all of it, that she needed right now. They could give her something later to take care of the infection.

"I'm okay," she whispered back." I think I'm catching a cold, that's all." She snuffled to reinforce her statement and wrapped her arms tightly around her chest. Indeed, the heat of her body accompanied by the shivering she felt made her think that there was some truth to her own words.

"Okay, then." Mike touched the device in his hand and the holo came to life.

Good evening Dr Carson. Thank you for being willing to talk so late in the evening. I'd like to introduce you to my granddaughter.

The holo of Dr Mallard turned to his left and reached out an arm to someone out of sight of the projector. Then a woman, almost as tall as him, with honey brown hair walked into view to stand beside him.

Nita screamed with excitement and half jumped out of her chair before she sank back overwhelmed by dizziness. "That's Julia Jewel, that's …"

Then she understood. She stared with shock at the stunning woman standing next to Dr Mallard and then turned her head to look at Mike who was in turn looking at her with confusion.

"But I thought you knew," he said, a bewildered look on his face. "Oh Gods, her body… the decomp … and we never told you on the ship. I thought …" Mike quickly touched the pad to pause the holo.

Nita's voice quavered. "That's our Julia?" She looked towards Mike for answers. "But I just saw one of her concerts last week. How?" She looked at Mike asking with her eyes for him to make sense of it all for her.

"Time delay," he explained. "They've been holding off letting her public know, running these archived concerts, until all of us have the full story and can figure out how to spin it."

"Julia Jewels is dead!" Nita dropped her face into her hands in despair. "How could it happen?" Her sobbing increased in volume and intensity as all of the events of the last few months came down on her in a rush. It was just too, too, much. She wanted to go home.

Mike looked at her with total bewilderment on his face. "I'm sorry I didn't know you were a fan."

It was Nita's turn to look up at him with bewilderment. "It was Julia Jewels …" The expression on her face finished the sentence. *How could you not be a fan?*

Mike fumbled with the pad in his right hand. The holo momentarily disappeared and then restarted from the beginning. "Look," he explained. This is clearly a shock for you that we didn't prepare you for, and I'm really sorry about that." He reached out with his left hand to touch Nita who was now curled up in a ball, still crying inconsolably. "Nita, watch the holo, please. It will help you to understand what has happened."

After a few moments, Nita at last uncoiled herself and lifted her head to stare once again at the frozen image of Dr Mallard. She nodded and kept her eyes fixed on the holo.

Mike took this as an indication to continue and started the holo again.

Good evening Dr Carson. Thank you for being willing to talk so late in the evening. I'd like to introduce you to my granddaughter.

Once again, the image of Dr Mallard reached out to his left to pull Julia Jewels into view of the camera. This time, Nita simply wrapped her arms tighter around herself and drew in a deep breath.

You of course recognize my granddaughter from her stage appearances. She's gotten quite famous over the last few years.

The image of Dr Mallard wrapped an arm around the image of Julia and gave her an affectionate hug.

But I can't imagine that you also know how much she has been involved with the development of our AI, Ruby. She's been in my lab with me from the very beginning. Her voice was the first one that we mapped for Ruby.

The holo of Julia Jewels hugged her grandfather affectionately. *I love Ruby.* she said.

Nita sighed. The sound of Julia's famous deep-throated response sent shivers down her spine.

And I think the feeling is mutual. Which is why I wanted to have this conversation.

Look, I know you're busy. So, for once in my life, I will try to make this brief. Julia and I had a conversation last night that got me to thinking about something. Julia, why don't you explain to Dr Carson what you shared with me last night?

Dr Mallard's image turned to Julia's and gave her a nod of encouragement.

Okay. Like my grappa said, I adore Ruby. And I told grappa last night how I wished Ruby could experience what it's like when I give a concert. The thrill I feel, the bit of fear right before it starts, and how I feel when I see all of my adoring fans. Its just so, so wonderful.

She paused and turned towards her grandfather. He nodded back at her with encouragement. The mutual affection between the two of them was evident.

Okay, so I asked grappa last night why we don't enhance AIs like the way we enhance humans. That is, everyone … except me of course … have sprockets so that we can access information from the AIs. We're enhanced to combine our cognitive capabilities with that of these thinking machines.

But what about the AIs? Ruby is really smart, and I love her. We grew up together and she's like a sister to me. But as smart as she is, she really can't feel the things that I feel. I try to explain to her how I feel during a concert but that's not the same as actually feeling it. So, I asked grappa why we couldn't use the sprockets in reverse to let Ruby experience what I'm experiencing?

Dr Mallard put his arm around Julia's shoulders, squeezed her gently and then kissed her on the cheek while whispered something in her ear outside the range of the recording.

I'll take it from here honey. Dr Carson and I have something to talk about that's a bit technical.

As Nita watched, still in awe at the proximity, even virtual, to her idol, Julia shot a smile in her direction and walked out of range of the projection. At the same time, the camera followed Dr Mallard as he moved across the room and sat in a chair similar to the one that Nina was now sitting in.

She's remarkable, isn't she? And that's why we need to talk a great deal more about what needs to be done and why. Dr Carson, you've done remarkable work with Ruby already. And I thank you for that. Our ability to apprehend terrorists and other thugs after attacks has increased exponentially and I'm sure that its doing great things to deter future attacks. But its not really enough and not really what our prime objective has been.

He paused and glanced down at his hands clasped in his lap. He appeared to be thinking about how to say something. Then he looked up with an expression of determination that surprised Nita who had become caught up in the tenderness between grandfather and granddaughter, something she would never experience.

Julia is right, in her own special way. We're still missing the emotional component, the EQ, in the way that our AIs interact with us. In spite of all the technological advances since I invented the sprockets, they still haven't brought the peace that I have yearned for. If anything, they have only made things worse as their power has been turned against us. I honestly believe that Julia, in her songs, has done more to increase harmony and cooperation between humans than all the billions upon billions of computations of all the AIs around the world.

The image of Dr Mallard paused again and leaned forward. If possible, there was even more intensity and determination in his expression.

Dr Carson, if what we're doing now isn't good enough, let's try something different. Let's follow Julia's idea and build an approach to enhance our AI. Let's give Ruby a soul. Let's modify my sprockets technology so that Ruby can directly experience what Julia is experiencing. Not Julia of course at the beginning. But after we've perfected the interface, then yes, I believe that Julia, in all her goodness, could impart to Ruby the insights into how to do good and not just eliminate evil.

The holo disappeared and Nita found herself looking across blank space toward the scientists sitting across the room from her. She turned to look at Mike, expectantly.

"The rest was just technical stuff that wouldn't really help you understand what we're doing here." he explained.

Mike put the pad back in his leg pocket and looked across the room at his colleagues. "Bill, why don't you share with Nita everything that has followed after that initial conversation?" He leaned back, apparently grateful to turn the floor over. As he did so, he took a look at Nita who was visibly shaking and then turned to the woman in the chair next to him and whispered something in her ear. The woman nodded and then quietly got up and left the room.

Bill cleared his throat. He too, it appeared, like several of the other individuals in the room was visibly affected by the sight of Julia.

"For the last three years or so we've been working almost exclusively on giving Ruby access to the human amygdala and hippocampus. Its by far the hardest thing we've ever done, and it's been only because of Ruby's unique architecture based on Rosehip neurons that we've been able to make progress."

Bill looked around the room as heads nodded in affirmation to what he was saying. "This may not mean anything to you Nita, but the reason that sprockets are so unique is because Dr Mallard found a way to link the technology to Rosehip neurons in the cerebral cortex. Ruby is the first, and we think and hope only, AI build on that same technology. Those patents are the most closely guarded in the universe."

"Anyway," he continued. "About a year in, we developed some prototypes and began preliminary testing on some subjects ..."

Nita looked around as she noticed a distinct restlessness and squirming among the individuals in the room. What was Bill trying to say?

Bill cleared his throat and looked down at the floor. "We lost six really good people, our friends actually, before we figured out what was wrong. The new interface couldn't be used with anyone who already had sprockets."

"We discovered the hard way that there was already too much compromise to the Rosehip network from the previous jacking that prevented the new mapping to take place. We had to work with individuals who had never been jacked, individuals without sprockets."

Julia, a voice in Nita's head shouted at her.

As if reading Nita's thoughts, Bill responded. "Not Julia at first, but we obviously got there." He dropped his head and stared at the floor. Eventually, after a few seconds, he lifted his head and looked directly at Nita. "You need to know this Nita, you need to know the truth of what we did to get to where we are now and why you are so important."

As if gasping for air, he gulped and then began again. "We used unwilling test subjects. Something we have never done before, and I swear to God that we will never do again. We chose foreign terrorists grunts, captured by our troops in Venezuela. They were already scheduled for execution, so we rationalized that what we were doing was okay, even though it wasn't. We used three in all. The first one, it fried his brainstem and he died within hours. The next one better. He lived a good week before his autonomic nervous system shut down. And then the third .... We barely had time to disable him before he had gained access to Ruby and overridden the communication protocols. We're still not sure if he communicated any information. But we knew then that we had it. That's when we contacted Dr Mallard with the news and asked him if his granddaughter still wanted to directly share her experiences with Ruby."

While he was talking, two additional figures in pale blue tunics and pants walked in and moved to stand behind Nita's chair. They both looked questioningly towards Mike who was holding Nita's arm and looking down at the swollen red circles around her sprockets.

Mike lifted his right arm, signaling to Bill. "Everyone," he said, "Nita's not well. We need to stop now and get her to a med station."

Mike stood up and turned to stand in front of Nita attempting to pull her up by the arms.

She fell back, unable to stand on her own. "Help," she mumbled and sank into unconsciousness.

CHAPTER 7

"So, what is it?" Mike asked impatiently, moving forward from where he was standing, waiting in the corner. He watched in horror as they lowered Nita's unconscious body onto a diagnostic table in the med station. "Did that butcher not bother to sterilize his work? That pig …"

"Its not that, Mike. It's something else." Strong arms pushed Mike back toward the door and out into the hallway. "Please, let us find out what it is. You'll know as soon as we do."

Mike stared as the door closed in front of him, then turned and almost bumped into Bill and several of the other members of his team … of Nita's team. They uniformly shared his look of worry and concern.

"What is it?" one of the team asked.

"They don't know." Mike said, increasingly aware of what that meant. *How could they not know?*

"They won't know for a while. Let's go back to the lounge and wait." Mike led everyone down the hall to the next section of the facility and the common areas.

Halfway down the hall Mike and his team were met by a group dressed for military combat.

"Dr Carson?" one of the men asked as he stepped forward.

Mike nodded, momentarily confused. Then he remembered. "Do you have the body?"

"Yes, sir."

Mike then thought of what the doctor had just told him, or rather, not told him. "Is it quarantined? It's got to be quarantined."

"Yes, sir. All taken care of, sir."

"Good. Make sure it stays that way."

Mike then thought for awhile and turned to the rest of the team. "Look, I've got to go back and let the docs know that we have Julia's body. I'll meet up with you later."

He quickly turned then and ran down the hallway back in the direction of the med station. Something told him that letting Nita's docs know about Julia's body was incredibly important. At the door to the med station he only hesitated a moment and then burst through.

"God dammit, Mike! I told you we would let you know once we figure this out. Get the hell out!"

Mike stopped in front of one of the men who he assumed was the head doctor and threw his hands up. "Listen. They just brought Julia's body in. They've got it in quarantine. There may be a connection."

Two of the doctors looked at each other and then back at Mike. Mike's guess was right as the doctor he was speaking to stepped away from the console and began giving directions. "Ferris," he said with authority, "Split off a separate team and go with Mike. We need to see if there is a connection."

* * * * *

Mike was asleep, stretched out on one of the couches in the commons room, when a hand shook his shoulder. Groggily, he opened his eyes to see one of the doctors from the med station looking down at him. "What time is it?" he asked as he pulled himself into a seated position, rubbing his eyes.

"Three-thirty, I've got good news for you and some not so good news. Which do you want first?" The doctor pulled a chair around to face Mike still sitting on the couch.

Mike shrugged. "Good, I guess."

"Well, we found out what it is. And it's the same for both of them. An extremely sophisticated neuro toxin. It's definitely what killed Julia and damn near killed Juanita. Once we found it in Julia's remains, it was relatively easy to find the minute strains in Juanita. And believe me, we were close to the point of no return. If she had been anywhere but here, she would be gone now."

Mike rubbed his temples, trying to force consciousness into his foggy brain. "A neurotoxin? Do you know the strain? What is it?" His brain spit out question after question.

The doctor sitting across from him reached out an arm and placed a hand on Mike's shoulder. "Look, I wish I could tell you more, but we just don't know. We've never seen this stuff before and its nasty. All we can tell is that it's distantly based on the herpes zoster virus, the one that causes shingles of all things. We're doing everything we can to figure out what it is. We also think that it might be related, a precursor perhaps, to the Neuro-Blast toxin that we've heard rumors about."

"But she's okay?" Mike asked.

"Yes, she's stabilized and as near as we can tell there is no neural or otherwise damage."

A surge of relief swept through Mike as he listened to the doctor's words. "Well at least you've cured Nita. Thank the Gods for that. I can't thank you enough."

The doctor stared at Mike with a confused look on her face. "Mike, you don't understand. We haven't cured her. The toxin is still in place. We've neutralized it temporarily but its still there, waiting to be triggered again. It's bonded to the Rosehip neurons and we don't know how to purge it from her body."

"And that's the bad news, right?" Mike asked, suddenly aware that anyone who was waking him up at 3:30 in the morning must have another, even more important reason for doing so.

The expression on the doctor's face spoke as much as her words. "No, it's far worse. We know the toxin is man-made and targeted to Julia's unique tech and consequently Nita's. Whoever poisoned her knew what she was and had to know all about us. We've been exposed. And we've been exposed for quite some time."

* * * * *

"But they may not know about Nita." Mike explained. The stim was still sitting in front of him in its small flask. He had reached out to it three times already and then pulled his hand back each time. Sure, it would work for a few hours, but then the payback would be hell. And he couldn't afford to pay that price for the next few days. So instead, he reached out for the mug in front of him with his old standby, coffee.

They were sitting in the conference rom where they always met to discuss important issues. A holo of Dr Mallard hovered at the front of the table.

"Is she alright?" Dr Mallard asked.

"She's fine, just a little tired, and she'll be joining us any time now." Mike explained.

The lead doctor from the med station, sitting opposite Mike at the table, leaned forward, directing his words to Dr. Mallard. "We only know a little about what the neuro toxin is, and we've got a pretty good idea of what it does and how it works. It acts similar to a herpes zoster virus, attacking the nerve ending but rather than moving down the pathways to the xxxxx, it moves in the opposite direction toward the spinal cord and into the brainstem itself. Its nasty and lethal and we can't cure it, but we've at least figured out a way to block it. We'll have something we, or she, can jack into her cranial port in a few hours. That way, if she gets attacked again, we have a chance of blocking it."

Even with his own medical training, a conversation far too medical for Mike to completely follow started between Dr Mallard and the lead doctor. As they were talking the door to the conference room slid open and Nita walked in. Mike saw her and patted the empty chair next to him. She quietly slid into the chair as Dr Mallard continued describing the unique characteristics of the sprockets technology and possible safeguards that could be put into place.

Dr Mallard paused in his lengthy explanation as he caught sight of Nita moving across the room to sit next to Mike.

"I'm sorry, is this Juanita who has walked in?" His face was alight with curiosity as he took a half step forward and looked intently in her direction.

Mike shoved his own chair back to give Dr Mallard a better view of Nita and pointed to her as he spoke. "Dr Mallard, let me introduce you to Juanita Yamashita, our extremely unlikely recipient of Julia's tech."

One of the members of his team coughed and half-raised his hand from where he was sitting near the front of the room. Mike looked at the man with confusion as he continued to motion to Mike for a chance to speak.

"What is it, Duncan?" Mike asked, somewhat perturbed by his impatient colleague's interruption of Dr Mallard.

Duncan looked at Mike who directed him with a hand wave to point his comments towards Dr Mallard. "Well," he began, "We've been working with Ruby since Julia failed her first check in. At first, we didn't understand what she was telling us … that is, until we heard about Nita." He paused and looked back at Mike who gave him the hand signal to speed things up.

"Anyway, it seems that Julia was sick for a lot longer than we knew … and she and Ruby actively worked to hide it from us."

"Why??" Dr Mallard looked back and forth between Duncan and Mike. "Why would they do that?"

Duncan's voice quavered nervously as he continued, unaccustomed to being with the major players. His words came rapidly. "We think it was because they didn't know how to cure Julia and had to find a way to save the project. As near as we can tell, we think that Julia and Ruby secretly worked to find her replacement. We're pretty sure that Julia and Ruby positioned her last moments to be at the edge of the dump where Nita's brothers would be sure to find her. They picked Juanita. It was no accident."

Stunned silence surrounded them. Even the faint buzz of the holo seemed to disappear. Then everyone, one by one, turned to stare at Nita.

* * * * *

Mike and Bill found a table in the atrium apart from the few other people who were still there mid-morning. The late autumn sun filtering through the dome felt good on Mike's back and he absently realized that apart from running back and forth to and from his car, he had not been outside for over two weeks. It occurred to him then in a flash that that the same could be said for Nita. My God, he realized, she's lived outside her entire life, virtually on the beach. He would have to find a way to get her outside as soon as possible ... and not in a parking lot.

He wasn't sure if taking a break was a good idea given his sleep-deprived condition, but it did give him an opportunity to grab another cup of coffee. As he looked around, he couldn't help but notice the additional uniformed presence evenly distributed around the perimeter. Even when they had walked out of the conference room a few minutes ago there were four armed guards standing there. It sent a chill up his spine to think about the implications that even the sun on his back couldn't counter.

"Mike, are you listening to me?" Bill's words penetrated Mike's brain fog.

"Sorry, just reflecting on all the military presence." Mike apologized. "What were you saying?"

Bill leaned forward as he spoke in a low tone. "I said, it's making me feel really uncomfortable, what Ruby is able to do now like finding Nita. That's pretty powerful stuff. Mike, I checked, Nita's not on our tagged list. I asked and no one has even heard of her. She's nowhere on any list, good or bad. So how did Julia and Rosie find her without adding her to any kind of watch list? How are they keeping secrets? And what other secrets are there that we don't know about?"

Mike leaned forward too and wrapped his hands around his coffee cup. "Predictive algorithms. Big data. We've never really tested the extent of Ruby's capabilities. That was sorta Julia's domain."

"That's the point, Mike. Look. AIs have been part of our lives since the day we were born, before that even, if my mum is right. Once we got our sprockets it was even more so. But we've always used the AIs in a specific way. We ask them questions, they give us answers. We ask them for information, they provide it. We ask them to make decisions, they make better informed decisions than we do.

They make us better. And that's how you and I and the rest of the team have been using Ruby."

Bill leaned even closer in across the table. "Mike, I gotta ask myself, what's in it for Ruby?"

Mike looked down at his empty coffee cup and pushed it around on the table. He sighed and looked up. "That's been Julia's domain. That's the whole point of this project, to let Ruby know what it's like to be a human."

"Yeah, I guess." Bill sat back and looked around the room, studying the armed presence. "But one more question for you, Mike. Who killed Julia? You know, I swear that Mallard knows but isn't saying."

Mike exchanged looks with Bill. His instincts were telling him the same thing. Raymond Mallard knew more than he was telling. And like Bill, Mike didn't know why he wasn't sharing.

CHAPTER 8

Director Walker stood up from his desk as his admin brought Secretary Mary MacIntosh into his office. If possible, the woman was thinner than the last time he had seen her two months ago when he had stood in front of her Pentagon desk trying to explain the loss of their most important asset. Her custom deep blue raw silk suit hung from her shoulders as if it were carelessly thrown onto a hanger of the wrong size.

"Mary, good to see you. I was hoping you would respond to our abbreviated communication. Would you like something to drink, tea, coffee?" Director Walker pointed her to a small conference table next to the window with several chairs.

"No time Frank. Let's make this quick. What the hell is going on? I couldn't tell if you were telling me good news or bad." She moved in long strides to the table and sat down in a jerky motion. Frank quickly followed behind her and took a chair opposite. There were no tablets or notebooks on the table between them. Each knew that the other had already started to record the meeting on their own private streams.

Frank took a deep breath. Meetings with Secretary MacIntosh always felt more like a knife fight than a dialogue. He had five minutes at the most to make his case. Mary had been known to get up in the middle of a presentation and walk out saying 'time enough' as she moved through the door.

"Okay, here it is. Julia's dead."

Secretary MacIntosh leaned forward, interrupting. "The pretty singer, right?"

"Yes, Dr Mallard's granddaughter, as you may remember."

"One of the dumbest decisions you've ever made." MacIntosh interrupted again. She then waved a boney hand, loosely circled by a half a dozen gold bracelets, indicating to hurry up.

"Okay. This is where it gets strange. A bunch of kids on Virgin Gorda in the ICVI found her decomposing body in a dump." Frank paused for just a moment to see if MacIntosh would interrupt again. Then quickly resumed as she waved her hand again.

"The story is that they brought the body home, stripped out Julia's tech and then went over to Tortola and found some pirate tech shop to jack it into the girl. And the damned stuff worked."

Mary sat back in her chair and put both hands up to stop Frank's explanations. "Okay, let me get this right." she said with a tone of implicit disapproval. "There is some island mongrel girl now wandering around with a half billion dollars of our tech in her body?" Her eyes rolled up into her head and then returned to center intently on Frank.

"Not wandering. She's here." Director Walker quickly said. "Two of my best men went down and grabbed her. She's been here for almost a month."

Frank expected Macintosh to drill him again. But instead the secretary closed her eyes and started twitching her fingers. She was checking her stream for something. As Secretary of Defense her sprockets included several terabytes of additional internal processing capabilities stored on a subcutaneous unit. Frank squashed the image in his brain of where they could possibly have found a place on her boney body to mount it.

When she opened her eyes again there was actually a small smile on her face. "Frank, you realize that this could actually be fantastic news. We could finally be out from under the grip of that mad scientist Mallard for good."

Frank smiled back. He too, over the last 24 hours had realized the same thing. As long as the project was centered around Mallard's granddaughter there had been precious little influence he could exert on the direction of the work. Now, though, with that factor removed, they could take the research in the direction that was their secret intention.

"Can I see her?" MacIntosh asked. "Now?"

Frank hesitated. He didn't want the secretary to know about the neurotoxin incident just yet and he wasn't sure what condition Nita was in. "Let me check to see where she is." Frank said. Unlike MacIntosh he left his eyes open as he twitched his fingers to access the building directory which quickly overlaid his sight. Relieved, he saw that Nita and her two brothers were in one of the labs with several of his techs including Mike and Bill.

"They're in one of the labs now with our team. It's about a ten-minute walk from here." He was already out of his chair and motioning the secretary to follow him. Experience told him that when the secretary wanted something it was best to act quickly.

* * * * *

Director Walker was out of breath trying to keep up with the Secretary as they marched down the hallway pushing aside more casual walkers along the way. The NAA Behavioral Institute was a maze of labs and the fact that only Director Walker knew where they were going kept their pace to less then a dead run.

Walker finally stopped in front of a double panel door and paused to look through the glass panels first before opening it. He could see a cluster of white-coated staff huddled around Nita who was sitting in front of a large holo panel. To his chagrin, her brothers were also in the room peaking around the staff to get a look at what Nita was doing.

He took a deep breath and pushed the door open. "Gentlemen," he announced with outspread arms. "I have a fantastic surprise for you. Secretary MacIntosh is here to see the work we are doing … and of course to introduce herself to our Nita."

The lab hadn't been particularly noisy before but now it came to total silence as heads turned toward the duo at the door. Secretary

MacIntosh pushed passed Director Walker and strode to the holo panel pushing aside people as she went.

"So what are we doing here?" she asked, taking in the familiar blue filament extending between the holo panel and Nita's neck sprocket. "Are we talking to the RBY-8?"

Mike stepped up positioning himself protectively next to Nita's chair. "Secretary MacIntosh, thank you for your visit. No, we're just beginning to teach Nita here how to use her sprockets. So right now, we're only giving her access to one of the peripheral lab computers to teach her how to interface."

"But they work?" secretary MacIntosh asked, now taking a serious look at the girl at the other end of the blue filament. "She's fully functional, right? So how long is all this interfacing going to take before you jack her into the RBY-8?"

Mike, unlike his boss Director Walker, wasn't comfortable with the knife-like dialogue coming from the Secretary. He stammered but then caught a look from his boss that 'encouraged' a rapid response. "She's really bright," he said. "She's learning quickly, and I estimate that we'll be introducing her, slowly of course, to the RBY-8 within a week."

"Well she damn well should be bright. She's got half a billion of our tech inside her." Secretary MacIntosh didn't wait for a response. She gave Nita one more fierce look and then turned on her heels and strode toward the door with the director hastily following her.

As she was leaving, she started up a conversation with the director behind her. "What the hell are they?" she asked." Is that some sort of mongrel Jap and Black mix?"

"Not quite," Director Walker gasped as he paced behind her. "Their dad's Jap but their mom is Carib Indian from what I'm told."

Secretary MacIntosh stopped in her track, apparently recognizing that she was moving at an accelerated pace in a direction without a known destination. She turned and faced the director. "So, they're not NAA citizens?"

"No, of course not. They're residents of the ICVI." Director Walker explained again. "I suppose you could say that we kidnapped them."

Secretary MacIntosh played with her left earring as she thought for a moment. Then she smiled. "Good. Perfect. Weaponize the hell out of her. I want a weekly report. … And get rid of those mongrel brats with her. And one more thing. Keep that witch off sproc-net and away from all those damn anarchists." She paused for a moment as she scanned the unfamiliar hallway they were in. "And show me the way out of this damn rat's maze."

* * * * *

As the door closed behind the exiting director and the secretary, several conversations started simultaneously In the lab. That was good for Nita who unnoticed, turned her attention and her heightened hearing to following the conversation on the other side of the doorway. *Weaponize? Mongrel Brats?* She wanted to ask Mike but quickly realized that she had other options. She ran her fingers down the thin blue filament and in spite of her fear smiled. There were now other ways to get information.

CHAPTER 9

The community room, the 'lounge' as the people here called it, was relatively quiet. Most people had gone home to their families living in the small suburban communities in the vicinity. Only those few who lived her in the facility or were working late remained. Nita and her two brothers were able to solely occupy one corner of the room, closest to the biggest holo screen in the space.

Nita continued to be amazed at how comfortable Jorge and Pepe were with the tech. Right now, they were competing with each other, trying to be the first to integrate their brand-new G-cubes with the holo screen suspended from ceiling struts.

It felt strange to Nita in so many ways to be here. Her own tech of course created a newness to everything she experienced. But there was something else too. It was about time, having too much of it. to be precise. She hadn't really thought about how she had used time before. If she was awake, she was working. It was as simple as that.

Now however, it was different. Just sitting here with nothing that needed to be done felt strange and uncomfortable. She thought about just the last few hours after most of the team had left for the day. After they were gone, she and her brothers had wandered down to the cafeteria for dinner. She didn't have to go out to the garden and pick vegetables, prepare the meal and serve it. And when they were done, there was no kitchen to clean up.

She looked at her brothers again. They were so happy just playing. When had she lost the ability to play? It was so long ago that she couldn't remember. Ever since their mother died and their father deserted them, every waking moment had been absorbed with the effort to keep the three of them alive. She shuddered then remembering the words of the scrawny woman with the black aura, *mongrel brats*, she needed to talk to Mike about that – and do her own research.

She reached down to pick up the new pouch she had been given by one of the doctors. Her 'kit' was what the doctor had called it. The fabric was a light tan color and soft to the touch, just like so much of this new world seemed to be. She pulled back the front flap and looked at the numerous small pockets on the front. Inside several of them were blue filaments like the ones she had used in the lab today and ever earlier in Ernesto's shop on Tortola.

But some were decidedly different. With her enhanced vision she could detect the slight differences even though the doctor had said that for anyone without her enhanced vison they would be indistinguishable. She gently pulled one of the fatter and deeper blue coiled filaments from its pocket and held it in her hand. It shimmered slightly.

"Is that what I think it is?" a voice came from her right side. She turned her head and found Mike sitting next to her.

"Our medical team told me that they had developed a delivery system using filament technology. But this is the first time that I've seen it." Mike reached out his hand and lightly touched the blue filament coiled in Nita's palm. "Amazing, just amazing."

"This is all so new to me." Nita confessed. "So much is changing and so fast." It was true. And as Nita sat there with nothing to do but think about it, it was beginning to crash down around her. Even in the over-warm and airless room, she found herself shivering. "I miss the ocean and the sun." she confessed.

Mike leaned forward and put his hand softly on her shoulder. "Look," he said, "I've been thinking about it too. How you're cooped up in this building when you've lived your entire life out of doors. How about if I negotiate a trip of some kind? Get us out of here?"

"With my brothers?" Nita asked, her mind leaping forward to the thought of being outdoors again.

"No, let's leave them here this time. I think they know how to keep themselves occupied." They both laughed as they watched the boys who were now engaged in a holo battle in what appeared on the screen to be the asteroid belt. Nita however, also felt a sense of dread at the thought of being away for too long from her brothers. *Mongrel brats.*

*****

Time continued to bewilder Nita. She was in her room, still awake and not tired even though it was perfectly dark outside the single window looking out onto the grassy park that formed the hub of the hexagonal building complex.

She supposed that she should go to bed as Mike had recommended. He said that they would have a busy day tomorrow. But there was something that she wanted to do first, that she needed to do first before she could sleep.

She walked over to the desk and sat down in front of the screen. There was already a blue filament sitting on the table beside the screen. She picked it up and reached around to snap it into her neck port the way she had been instructed today. Then, just like she also practiced today, she snapped the other end into the bottom of the panel.

Good. The now familiar NAA-BI display appeared. She subvocalized her personal information, her 'account' they called it.

Just like it had happened in the lab today, a voice 'spoke' to her from inside her head. *'What would you like to do today, Nita?'*

Mike had told her that this was the most primitive form of AI interaction that they were starting with, what lower school children first learned in the elite prep schools.

Query, she subvocalized. *Definition for weaponize.*

The response flashed on the panel in front of her and echoed inside her head. *Weaponize, transitive verb, to adapt for use as a weapon of war.*

So, she thought. They were somehow planning to turn her into a weapon of war. Somehow that didn't surprise her. Deep inside she already knew the truth of it. Did they do the same thing to Julia? Was that how she got murdered?

Thinking about Julia she felt a pang of sadness. Julia Jewel was her one and only idol in the world. She dreamed sometimes about being Julia. Now, was she actually ....

Sproc-net. Julia Jewel fanpage. Without consciously realizing what she had done, Nita found herself staring at Julia's fanpage. She quickly noticed that there was still no mention of her disappearance and death. Instead there were images of her most recent concert from last week, a new song to download, and tons of gossip about her romantic interests.

There was also a new blinking light on the messages icon that wasn't there the last time Nita logged in from the kiosk in the Valley parking lot. Probably just another mass mailing announcing a new event. Nita almost deleted it without opening, but on an impulse opened the message anyway.

In front of her a holo image of Julia Jewel walked out of the panel and sat on the edge of the desk, dangling bare legs and feet. The desk and the corner of the room were overlaid with what looked like the landing at Spring Bay back home.

> *"Nita, I do, so, so, hope that's you that I'm sharing this message with. How are you my dear? This is Julia Jewel, unfortunately as I hope you already know, sending you a message from the grave.*
>
> *Look dear, I'm not sure how to explain this in a way that doesn't positively drive you over the edge. But here it goes. Like I said, I'm dead. This message was sent to you just before my death while my neural pathways were still functioned reasonably well.*
>
> *So... here goes ... by now I hope that your two brothers have found my body at the dump. If they haven't then you need to send them right now this very instant to go collect it and bring it back home. Its on the northern edge about 100 meters from the beach wall.*

> *Now dear, here's the gruesome part. I of course have sprockets. But mine are different. They are very, very special sprockets. And guess what – I'm giving them to you! But this is where it gets yucky. You'll need to remove them from my body – wrists and back of neck too. Oh, and make sure you get the chip inside my head, right at the back, very, very important.*
>
> *Now here's the tricky part. Ruby and I, she's my very special AI, decided that the best thing for you to do was to get them jacked somewhere on Tortola. Do not, my dear, I repeat, do not contact the NAA and just turn them over. No, you've got to get them jacked into you so that those horrible folks at NAA can't take them away from you.*
>
> *We've heard that Ernesto's on Tortola does the best work but that could be really dangerous. Ruby has been able to build a predictive model that gives you about a 70% success rate for getting my sprockets implanted successfully jacked into you. And about a 50% success rate of successfully getting off Virgin Gorda and finding your way to the NAA research facility.*
>
> *Which leads us, Nita dear, to the real importance and urgency of this message.*

Nita sat mesmerized as she watched Julia's projection stand up and walk back toward the beach. And yes, it definitively was Spring Bay back home. Nita drew up her knees and wrapped her arms around them to contain the trembling that was spreading through her body. *Julia, Julia Jewel was actually talking to her!* She watched in amazement as Julia stopped and sank down onto the sand.

> *I'm so tired Nita, so incredibly tired. So, you need to really listen to me. I am so, so, sorry for the burden that I am placing on you and how I am turning*

your life upside down and inside out. But whatever you do, you must, must, find a way to get my sprockets jacked and then just as importantly, you must, must find a way to get access to Ruby, my AI. That's the only thing that matters.

And then, if you can, you must find your way to my grandpapa Mallard. From there he will know what to do. Nita, grandpapa and I are committed to using this technology to improve the world we live in. But there are those who want to use it solely to accumulate personal power. You can't let them use you!

Julia's projection was now leaning back on her elbows, lying on her back in the sand. At the edge of the projection Nita could make out an automated salvage cart, the kind that picked up the commercial trash at the Spanish Town pier, rolling onto the beach. With horror she watched as the cart moved toward Julia. "No, no!" Nita cried, as sobs racked her body.

Nita, I'm afraid there isn't much more time. So, I need to say this quickly. We need you. We need you desperately. We're counting on you to complete our mission. I know that you can rise above your wildest dreams and become the woman who leads us to a better place. With your Kalinago background, you'll be able to integrate with Ruby in ways that I never could. Nita I am counting on you to not only protect this tech from getting into the hands of the bad guys but also to use it to make a positive change in the world. Please Nita …

If possible, Nita's horror increased as she watched the mesh scoop on the salvage cart drop down on the sand and push its way towards Julia's reclining body. Without realizing it Nita was shouting at the top of her lungs, "Stop it. No, that's Julia! Someone, save her!"

As the scoop slid under Julia and began raising upward to deposit her in the bin, one final message came from a weakened Julia.

> *Nita, I almost forgot, there is one person who can help you and explain more about our mission. Find Dr. Mike Carson at NAA-BI. Trust no one else. He's one of the good ...*

Nita screamed and sobbed at the same time as the projection ended. She looked, and the message was gone from her stream, apparently self-deleting. It was then that she became conscious of the pounding on her door and the yells from the other side. "Ms. Yamashita! Are you okay? This is security! Please open up or we'll come in!"

Still trembling, Nita uncoiled herself and took the few steps to the door. She opened the door a crack and peered out at the two massive guards in what to her untrained eyes, looked like full combat gear. Her chip confirmed her suspicions. "I," she stammered, making a show of rubbing her eyes. "I had a bad dream. I must have been talking in my sleep. But I'm okay now."

"You were screaming, ma'am. That must have been quite a dream." The two guards looked at her for a minute and then saluted. "You be careful there, ma'am."

"Thank you. I guess no horror vids before bedtime." Nita closed the door, and as an afterthought locked it, realizing at the same time what a useless gesture it was. She turned off the overhead lights and in the remaining light from the holo panel made her way to the bed and climbed in, pulling the duvet over her head.

Slowly it began to sink in. *Julia Jewel was counting on her, had picked her personally. It was Julia's truly dying wish that Nita, simple maker of goat cheeses from a small island in the ICVI, was to carry forward her mission. Julia trusted Nita. Julia believed in Nita. Julia was counting on Nita.*

Nita uncurled herself under the duvet and rolled onto her back with her arms and legs out straight. She opened her eyes and stared at the ceiling. "By the gods of my father and of my mother. By the

Amida Buddha and Kuan Yin, the goddess of compassion, of my father's lineage and by Nonu-ma the moon and Huoiou the sun, of my mother's lineage, I swear that I won't let you down, Julia." she said in a whisper. "You can count on me. I'll make you so proud of me."

CHAPTER 10

SOMETHING WAS GOING on. Mike could sense it. First, the announcement yesterday that the director would be gone for two days which, although a good thing in itself for everyone who was tired of having him hovering over their work, was strange in the way it was so publicly announced. And then today. Double it seemed of the amount of uniforms. Movements of equipment into the gym and courtyard and a general sense of busyness. Something was afoot.

But at least Nita was in a good mood, a startlingly good mood. She had positively raced into the lab this morning and was sprocketed before Mike even arrived. All of her hesitation and self-effacing uncertainty seemed to have vanished overnight replaced by some newfound inner confidence.

The call from the director's office arrived in the way of a building-wide broadcast just after the lunch break. Mike waved for Bill, who was sitting at a conventional panel with Jorge and Pepe, to step in and assist Nita with her training although frankly there was little additional help that she needed. He gathered his notepad and stylus and made his way to the director's office at the other end of the building. As he walked through the halls, he continued to see more activity as uniformed men and women moved about with a sense of urgency. Yes, something was definitely going on – and he had an uncomfortable feeling that he was about to find out what it was.

His suspicions were confirmed when he walked into Director Walker's office and found two additional individuals already seated in the chairs in front of the director's desk. A single chair remained open.

"Greetings, Mike. Please take a seat." Director Walker signaled to the empty chair. "I think you already know Dr Wayne Phillips from Analytics. And this is Coronal Andrew Hoffman."

As Mike was half-way seated in the chair, the Coronal quickly stood up and stretched a hand toward him in greeting. Awkwardly, Mike rose from his half-crouched position to shake the man's hand. The coronal grinned and returned to his seat. *You did that on purpose, you son of a bitch.* Mike realized as he finally sat down.

"Alright, I'll get to it. Mike, I've already briefed everyone on the project, so I just need to fill you in on the changes that will be happening." Director Walker sat back in his chair and hesitated. Mike sensed that the director was most likely calling up a prepared speech from his stream.

"Mike, as I've told Dr Phillips and Coronel Hoffman, our circumstances have changed dramatically. And as I've reflected on it, it's given us some opportunities to significantly improve our position. First, this truly bizarre course of events that has found Julia's tech now implanted into some random girl who is not even an NAA citizen means that we can now begin the process of getting ourselves out from under Dr Mallard's influence. We will no longer have to dance around our concerns for Dr. Mallard's precious granddaughter. We can now move toward our original intention for this facility."

"That's why Coronel Hoffman is here and has been read in. He's going to take over the role of Juanita's trainer. Her military and covert ops trainer."

Mike, stared, momentarily stunned. "But that's totally in opposition to Dr Mallard's wishes!" he interrupted. "That's exactly what he didn't want to happen with Julia or Ruby. He'll pull the plug on Ruby for sure."

The director templed his well-manicured fingers in front of his mouth. He didn't say anything to Mike about his interruption. But his eyes told the story.

"Well Mike," the director finally continued, spitting out Mike's first name like a projectile. "That too has changed along with the change in equipment, so to speak. The Secretary of Defense informed me yesterday that if we can commit to weaponizing the technology, and duplicate the effort so that we can, if not mass produce, at least have duplicates, then the department will be happy to fully fund us, including our expanded mission. We no longer need or want Dr Mallard's intrusions."

It wasn't lost on Mike that while the director was referring to him by first name, he was intentionally referring to his two new 'partners' by their titles. He recognized that he was on thin ice. But he had to try to save the program. "Director, forgive my insistence, but Dr. Mallard is the only person who fully understands Ruby. And as for replicating the tech, we tried that over a dozen times before with disastrous results. And we still don't know how Julia died, who poisoned her. Don't you think that we should solve that mystery before we launch into other projects."

Director Walker sighed. "Mike, that's exactly why Dr. Phillips is here. He's going to take the lead in backtracking Julia's trail to see if he can find the intersection where she got poisoned. We've got this covered. Tonight, he's going to sedate Juanita while she's sleeping and take a download from her implant. Once we integrate that with the RBY-8's information, that will give us the most recent images of who poisoned her."

Mike sat back in his chair stunned. "You can't. That goes against every principal that we stand by. Her personal records are sacrosanct. It's against the law, for God's sake!"

"Mike, Mike, Mike … we're at war. And as for the law, she's not even an NAA citizen. As far as records are concerned, she doesn't even exist." The director paused and shot a smile at Mike that sent a shiver up his back. "And if we want to get technical, it was you after all, Mike, that kidnapped her and her brothers."

Mike sat back, recognizing that he was temporarily defeated. He wondered how long he would have a job. And with what he knew … given the direction that the project had now taken …. how long did he have to live?

He needed to buy time to somehow get a message to Dr Mallard. "Okay, I understand" he said, with forced meekness, "… and I'll do whatever I need to do to be helpful." He shot a weak smile in the direction of Wayne and the coronel.

A chilling thought suddenly came to Mike's mind. He turned his attention back in the direction of Director Walker. "I have one more question if you don't mind."

"Of course, Mike, what else can we explain."

"I know we've made improvements in the chip tech since Julia came on board. But how are we going to find volunteers to try it out?"

"But Mike, you're not seeing the obvious." The director's voice had taken on the tone of someone tutoring a small, and not particularly bright, child. "We have two perfect subjects already. They know too much to ever let them leave this facility. They are young and healthy and without previous sprockets. And as I understand they have been asking for sprockets. Yes, Juanita's two brother will be perfect test subjects."

Mike's stomach roiled. He swallowed hard to keep bile from rising up into his mouth. His hands gripped the arms of the chair. He took a breath, futilely trying to calm himself. *Think, think ...*

As the Director finished up the details of the meeting and was dismissing everyone, Mike suddenly remembered something. "Oh, I'm sorry. One more thing that's important," he said, as everyone was shaking hands.

The director sighed, clearly impatient to end the meeting. "Alright Mike, spit it out."

"It's Dr Mallard, he's been calling daily requesting that Nita visit him in Maine so that he can get to know her and assess the condition of her sprockets. We can't keep ignoring him. At least for a while yet."

The director gave Mike another smile that sent a shiver up his back. "That's been taken care of Mike. We've arranged for Nita to take a two-day visit to him next week. We're not quite ready to make the shift away from his control on the project and we need to manage any suspicions that he might have. We also frankly need him to take a close look at Juanita. Security reported two nights ago that they heard her screaming in her room, calling out Julia's name. Given the problems that we had with all the previous implants, we want him to take a last look at her and see if he can provide some insights. You'll accompany her to take close notes for our further use."

As Mike moved to follow his colleague and the coronel out the door, Director Walker called him back. "Mike, stay for a minute. I have a few other things to discuss for just the two of us."

The door closed, and Mike was alone with the director who once again signaled for Mike to take a chair,

Once seated the director began. "I recognize Mike that this is a bit of a change for you and I am frankly extremely concerned that you are not fully onboard with the new direction we are taking."

Mike clutched the arms of the chair to keep his hands from shaking. "You're right, it is a big change for me but I'm sure that I'll be able to adjust."

"I hope that you are right. But in the words of early forces, 'Trust but verify.' All of your communications and actions are going to be monitored for at least a month until we can be certain that you are fully onboard with this new program. That especially includes all of your messaging with Dr Mallard. You'll be allowed to attend Juanita on her trip to visit Dr Mallard. Frankly, we still need your expertise as well. But anticipate an intensive questioning when you return. And don't forget, we still have our subjects brothers here if you or her think about doing anything stupid."

Mike looked at the director fully comprehending what had just been said. He translated 'intensive' to its implied meaning, *neural.* "I understand sir? Will that be all?"

The Director waved his hand, dismissing Mike who got up and shakily walked to the office door. Once past the outer door, he ran down the hallway until he could find a men's room. Inside, he found a stall and vomited again and again until there was nothing left. Even as he was emptying the contents of his stomach though, a plan was forming. He had to find a way to get to Bill and hope and pray that he would be onboard.

CHAPTER 11

FROM THE BACK seat of the helo, Nita looked down over the east coast of what used to be called the United States of America and was now part of the larger, more inclusive North American Alliance. The cloud cover was intense, and she only got occasional glimpses of the coast line. It was the greyness that surprised her. She felt a sense of depression settle around her as she looked out at the bleakness of the ocean. Where was the turquoise of the Caribbean that had been a part of every day of her life except for the last month?

"Why is it grey? Is the ocean sick?" Nita leaned to her right and yelled into Mike's ear.

He laughed. "Well that's actually two questions. Its grey because it's the Atlantic. All the oceans north and south of the equator are blue-grey in color. As for whether the ocean is sick, well you know that as well as I do. They're all sick. Even your beautiful Caribbean with its dead coral reels."

"Thanks," Nita sat back and again processed a new piece of information. It was all so incredibly strange to her. Just sitting here, bundled up in a heavy coat with a hood over her head and thick socks and mittens was totally alien to her. When in her life had she ever worn socks or mittens?

They were going to someplace called the Acadia National Park and Mount Desert island. And she was going to meet Dr. Raymond Mallard, the man who had invented her sprockets … and the man who was the grandfather of Julia.

She felt a bit nervous, but in comparison to how she felt less than a week ago, she was floating in a sea of calm blue water.

"Where's New York City?" she asked again. She really already knew the answer, but it felt good to be almost outside again and with people who weren't carrying guns. Every muscle in her body ached from the last week of intensive drills they had suddenly started putting her through. Climbing walls, lifting weights, even parachute drills – what was the point of that? She had tried to ask Mike for answers, but he had been surprisingly silent.

"Yeah," Mike leaned forward and smiled at Nita. "Look out the left window and you'll see the new land-based cities and the bridges. The entire eastern seaboard is of course one big metro complex now all the way almost to where we're going. All this directly below us is the sea plain. Kinda pretty, isn't it, in a sad sorta way. But wait until you see Manhattan Island. It looks really cool from up here like an inverted castle."

Nita looked out over the grey mud of the sea plain, not sure if she was remembering its description from the six years of obligatory schooling in Virgin Gorda or the chip working in the background. With the rising sea level all the communities on the eastern and western seaboards had given up on saving themselves. Instead, they had invested in massive relocation of their cities inland a hundred miles or more. All that is, except for New York City which had chosen to build the moat that surrounded the Island.

It was these moves, more than anything else, Nita remembered, either from school or her chip, that had led to the collapse of the old US. With all of the resources of the government focused on saving three coastlines, while the rest of the country sat neglected, baking and rotting in the rising temperatures, it wasn't long before political revolt led to Canada's acquisition of the central part of the US and the remainder of Mexico primarily as an act of compassion.

She sat back in her seat, overwhelmed by the newness of everything around her. Idly, she wondered how her goats and chickens were doing. Was Carmine alright, really alright? The team that had brought what was left of Julie's body back to the facility for examination, had said that everything looked fine. But how would they know? Who knew more about goats than she did? As she learned more about using her chip, she would have to find a way to check in on Carmine and see if there was any way that she could help her.

Her chip. Ahh, her chip. After her recovery, her team made the decision to start aggressively training her to use it. Not with Ruby, of course, but with another conventional AI used primarily for educational and business purposes. *Her team ... it seemed so strange to think of them that way.*

Over the last month she had finally come to realize that they really were mostly good people and that they genuinely cared for her well-being. Even the massive men, and women too, who for the past week were now taking her through physical drills to 'toughen her up' for three hours each morning were nice enough. Their massiveness she discovered through gossip with the rest of her team was due to genetic enhancements that their parents had 'volunteered' them for when they were still infants. In the uncertainty of NAA society, with the disappearance of public education and social services, the guaranteed placement of a son or daughter with the military or heavy industry seemed like a good bet to a family without a sprockets-implanted wage earner.

As she continued to look out the frosted window at the uniform greyness of the landscape below her, Nita wondered about her own future, and especially that of her brothers. She realized that for the past weeks she had for all practical purposes ignored her brothers. She had been far too absorbed in the changes going on in her own life. But what was the future going to be like for the two of them? Her newfound eidetic memory called back images from her peripheral vision of Jorge and Pepe sitting excitedly with Bill in front of computer panels. At the same time, it also brought back images of the past week of strange looks from her team, looks at both herself and her brothers. Even Mike seemed to be acting strangely. They knew something, she realized, that they didn't want to tell her. Something she suspect that was associated with the new morning rituals in the gym.

She shuddered as the realization sunk in.

"You okay?" Mike asked as he put an arm around her shoulder. "Are you cold? I can have the pilot turn up the heat."

"No," Nita said, deciding quickly not to disclose her concerns in front of the pilot. "I'm just wondering why all the coastlines and beaches are that grey-black color." She pointed out the window at the coastline below them.

"Oil," Mike explained. "And lots of other petrochemicals and toxins and stuff. It's gotten too expensive to clean up so they're just leaving it and treating it with some stuff that makes it inert and doesn't get reabsorbed back into the ocean. Promises are to clean it up in the future once there is more money for that kind of stuff."

A tear escaped from Nita's eye. One of the reasons for the establishment of the ICVI was the protection of what remained of the beauty of their surroundings. The ICVI had consciously chosen to become a haven for pirates and privateers as their major economic drivers if that meant saving themselves from the industrialization that was poisoning the rest of the planet. Even with dead and dying coral reefs, at least the ocean was still blue and the beaches white.

"It changes for the better once we get to Maine and the edges of the Acadia park where Dr Mallard lives." Mike explained. "That's when you'll see what winter is supposed to look like. There's snow and pines, and moose everywhere. Really, really pretty."

Nita turned and smiled weakly at Mike, even though tears continued to track down her checks. She remembered what Julie's last words were. *Trust Mike*. But then, what choice did she have? She was beginning to think that he was her only friend in the world and that frightened her more than everything new that she was experiencing with her sprockets. She had always fiercely taken care of herself and her brothers. And now she didn't know how.

Her thoughts came quickly back to the present as the first sights of New York City came into view below. To be precise, it was Manhattan Island that was below them, surrounded by a 50-foot-wide wall that extended on all sides. It was as if Nita was looking down into a massive well. Her sprockets told her that when standing in one of the streets below the wall it rose 50 feet into the sky above. The effect, depending on the time of day, was to leave a significant part of the city in shadows that were offset by grids of lighting that circles the inner sides of the sea wall.

Mike leaned over and shouted into Nita's ear even though with her augmented hearing it was unnecessary. "There are pumps that run through the entire structure so that if any waves come over with this hurricane that's heading our way, they can send the water back into the ocean again. They say that the cost of the engineers who built this structure doubled the Dutch GDP for ten years."

Nita looked out the window, now paying more attention to the darkening skies and the sound of the wind buffeting their helo. She could see the ocean, now almost black, starting to rise up in waves pounding the wall surrounding the city. A sense of foreboding came over her, not from her access to various newsfeeds through her sprockets, but from the gods of her mother. Silently, she mouthed a prayer for the local Icheiri to protect these people from the evil Maboya clearly present in the cresting waves.

* * * * *

An hour later the helo descended into a snow filled clearing. Close by, through a flurry of snow she could just see a large building made of a combination of the trunks of dead trees and large panels of glass. Standing midway between their helo and the building, a single man bundled in a surprisingly thin jacket and a multicolor knit cap, accompanied by the largest dog that Nita had ever seen, was waving at them.

In minutes, the doors to the helo were opened and Nita and Mike were standing in the blowing snow while they waited for the pilot to offload their two small bags from the back. The man from the house walked quickly up under the blades of the helo and grabbed Mike in a bear hug as best they could despite Mike's thick coat.

"Mike, I'm so glad that you could come with Juanita. I've heard such strange rumors this last week. I was afraid you wouldn't make it." The man released Mike after giving him a look foretelling further conversation. He then turned towards Nita who in spite of her thick coat was hopping up and down to keep warm.

"And this of course is beautiful, although clearly freezing, Juanita Yamashita! Welcome to Maine, Juanita! And Wonderland!"

The man who Nita now recognized as Dr Mallard reached out and gave her the same fierce hug that he had offered to Mike. It was impossible to resist the genuine warmth of his gesture and Nita returned the hug in kind.

"Come on, you two. Let's get to the house. We have to be mindful of Wolf, here. She's due to give birth any day now and I don't want her out in this cold for too long. Mike grab the sled."

The pilot had offloaded a small sled from the back of the helo and placed their bags on it. Mike walked back and grabbed the handle, activated the small motor, and started to walk to the house behind Dr Mallard and Nita who were now fully engaged in conversation. Behind them the helo took off and headed south.

"Glad you two got here!" Dr Mallard yelled over the sound of the helo taking off. "There's a grand daddy of a hurricane coming our way. A hurricane in Maine in the dead of winter, can you believe it! Got to get us into the house and everything battened down! Come on, Wolf, girl, before you have those pups right here in a snow drift."

* * * * *

Nita stared with both the freshness of newness and the sweetness of fond memories at the fire blazing in the hearth. This was a completely new experience for her and at the same time one that she had experienced tens of times before. This dual emotional resonance was something that she was becoming increasingly familiar with although not quite yet knowing how to reconcile.

Just minutes ago, Dr Mallard had directed the house computer that he called Sarah to raise the house shields. Nita had watched with that same mix of newness and oldness as massive walls of metal had risen from the ground outside the panoramic great room windows and continued upward until they meshed with other metallic sheets surrounding the rest of the house and grounds.

As the metallic-looking walls rose upward, the windows on either side of the fireplace had transformed into projection panels similar to the ones in the lower level. Scenes shifted across the panels as well as on additional screens above the fireplace from various positions outside the house displaying the metallic sheets that were now just beginning to seal together above the house.

Wonderland. That's what Dr Mallard had called this place, his home surrounded by endless snow, looking out at a grey, angry ocean. It was as strange to Nita, with her ingrained tropical island sensibilities, as if she were on another planet or in the lands of one of her gods.

Her thoughts were interrupted by the smell of chocolate and alcohol. Dr Mallard, now Papa Ray as he insisted that she call him, was standing beside her with three thick ceramics mug steaming on a tray between his hands.

"Careful," he cautioned as he handed her one of the mugs. "It's hot, so hold off a minute before you take a big sip."

With both hands, Nita held the mug under her nose and took in the aroma. Somewhere in her mind the word 'brandy' came forward. Again, a part of her didn't know what 'brandy' was and another part smiled with pleasure.

"That's it, just take in the aroma for a while as it cools off. That's exactly the way that my Julia used to hold her mug up to her nose." Dr Mallard sighed and walked over to where Mike was sitting and handed him the second mug from the tray. "Mike," he explained. "I gave you a double jigger just the way you like it. I don't forget important things like that."

"Thanks," Mike said as he took the mug and like Nita held it up to his nose to take in the fragrance. "Is that doing what its supposed to be doing?" Mike asked as he pointed to one of the screens with a blinking red light and displaying a single metallic panel that appeared to be stuck midway through its assent.

"Damn. That must be where a tree has come down on the side of the house. Thought I heard it crash into the house a few hours ago. But nothing we can do about it now."

Dr. Mallard shrugged, put the tray down on a small table next to the fire and took the final mug for himself. Like Nita and Mike, he took in the fragrance of chocolate and brandy before taking a cautious sip. "Ahh, perfect!" he exclaimed and took the seat in front of the fire between Nita and Mike. "The simple pleasures are always the best."

Together, they sat in silence for a few minutes savoring their surroundings. Then Dr. Mallard coughed and began to speak.

"Mike, I know you know this history and have no doubt heard it dozens of times, but I doubt that Nita has the whole story of how we've gotten to where we are and how I've come to live here. So, bear with me as I give her a version of history that I doubt she will ever see in a history stream."

Mike nodded in agreement and then slouched comfortably down in his chair and pushed his stocked feel closer to the hearth.

"Nita, a good deal of the blame for where we are right now needs to rest with me and my own ambitions. For that, I do apologize in advance. But perhaps after the telling you might feel a bit of compassion for me."

"Now then, I'm not sure how much NAA history you've read but in the early days of the NAA as everyone was struggling to figure out where to find the money to save cities like New York, Vancouver, San Francisco, and the like, funding for the national parks and monuments, not to mention schools and social services, completely dried up. The park service was too busy fighting forest fires and mud slides to care about keeping toilets and gift shops open in the parks. Then someone in the newly formed congress came up with the idea of selling the parks to organizations that could guarantee their care and maintenance for the privilege of using a portion of each park for their own personal pleasures. The National Park and Monument Stewardship Bill, as it came to be called, set out the procedures for selling off the NAA's most precious treasures to the highest bidders."

Dr. Mallard paused and took a sip of his brandy-laced hot chocolate. He looked into the fire as if he was back ten years ago standing in front of the senate. "That's when I made my deal with the devil." he said slowly.

"I was just coming into the immense wealth resulting from the sprocket technology and its global acceptance. I had more money than I knew what to do with. At that time, I was also in full swing working on the prototypes that would eventually become Ruby, the RBY-1 through RBY-7. I frankly was getting extremely nervous about the potential of my Rubys and how to protect them from industrial espionage. I needed a secure home for them. That's when I made my deal with the NAA. They didn't want just my money to purchase the Acadia National Park here. They wanted my technology too, as part of the going price. So, I made a deal."

Dr. Mallard paused and stared over his mug at the fire for several minutes. Nita, who had drawn her legs up under her in the chair, twisted around to look at Papa Ray.

"We made a deal," he said, finally breaking the silence. "… that I would fund what is now the Behavioral Institute as an arm of the Department of Defense. That was the part that I objected to venomously. I argued, and I was totally right, that the BI should be a part of the Department of Education. At that time, I was fully engaged with my work to bring the sprocket technology to as many people, and especially the disadvantaged, as possible and education for all was, and still is, my obsession. But the DOE was then, and still is, only a shadow of its former self. The public school system was in the process of being sold off at the same time that the park system was going the way of the Dodo. There was no money in the DOE budget to fill the funding gap to set up the facility I needed. Only the DOD had the funding to create the military and Intel level security that I needed at that time to protect my Rubys. So, I made a deal with the devil to give my newly developed Ruby-8 to the DOD and set up the facility where Mike now works and where you, dear Nita, have been held prisoner. That was eight years ago."

"Ironically, as soon as I took ownership of the land here, the first thing that I did was build this residence and its underground research facilities, carved into Maine granite, with security that would make the DOD cry with shame. That's where I began my work on Ruby-9. Which happens to be directly below our feet ..."

Surprising both Nita and Mike who were half-asleep in their chairs, Dr. Mallard leaped from his chair and spun around to face both of them holding his now empty mug up in the air. "And that's what I have been dying to show both of you since you got here!" he exclaimed with energy. "Get up you two lazy indolents! It's about time that you met Ruby -9!"

Dr Mallard strode between the chairs in the direction of the kitchen and stopped a few feet from the door when he noticed that he was not being followed. "Well come on, I'm serious. Follow me!" He waited half turned back toward the fireplace and the chairs surrounding it.

Nita was the first to move. She sat up straight, still holding her mug of chocolate and looked at Mike who was slower to return to full alertness. "Is he serious?" She asked him, gulping down the last of her chocolate.

"Why ask me," Mike said. 'Its his house and I guess he wants us to follow him." Mike then, following Nita's lead finished his own chocolate and put his mug down. "Let's go and see what he's so hot to show us." With that, he stood up, stretched and walked around his chair to catch up with Dr Mallard.

Nita did the same and soon they were shuffling into the kitchen on stockinged feet. Dr Mallard was already in the back of the kitchen standing inside a massive walk-in pantry. He looked behind him at Nita and Mike and then reached into one of the side shelves and began rearranging canned goods. "I can hardly wait until you see this." He grinned and then turned back around to stare at the rows of pantry shelves on the right … which were now receding into a previously hidden empty space behind the pantry.

Dr Mallard then took two steps to his right and disappeared out of sight. Nita and Mike looked at each other with puzzlement. Then Mike shrugged his shoulders and said, "What the hell," … and stepped into the pantry. As he too disappeared to the right, his voice echoed. "Well I'll be damned!"

Nita paused and then followed both of the men into the pantry. As she stepped forward into the same space an extremely bright light suddenly came from the right where both of them had disappeared. Its stark contrast to the soft diffused light of the house and the fireplace startled her.

As she turned to the right, she got a better understanding of what had happened. In front of her a polished metal ramp led down at a gentle angle along the walls of what appeared to be a large circular space. As she curiously took a few steps onto the ramp she could make out the space in front of her and below her. The ramp circled around half of a massive opening that appeared to be carved out of solid rock. Her internal processing instantly gauged the height of the room to be 24 feet and its diameter to range from 80 to 100 feet depending on where you stood. The shear size of it stunned her senses as she readjusted to the difference between the warmth and intimacy of the living room and hearth and this massive sterile environment.

Papa Ray and Mike were already most of the way around the ramp and about to move into the open space. She hurried her steps, wincing a bit as the metal of the ramp from time to time pressed through her wooly socks. But she was too amazed with what she was seeing to watch where she was stepping too carefully. She paused and peered over the railing to take everything in. In the center of the room there was a pit with another much smaller ramp circling around its inside wall. At the center of the pit a blue column of exactly the same color as the sprocket filaments she had grown so accustomed to, glowed and modulated. She had a powerful sense that it was alive and watching her, aware of her presence. *Was this actually Ruby?*

In one hemisphere of the room there was a single chair that reminded her of the chair in Ernie's shop where she had first gotten her sprockets. But as alike as these chairs were, they were even more different. This one was gleaming and silver with deep blue padding everywhere. Everything looked impossibly clean, just like her cheese making facility but brand new and not used like her own equipment.

Nita's absorption in her surroundings was broken by a laughing voice from below. "Are you coming, or do we have to come up there and pry you off the rail?"

"I'll be there in a minute." she called down to the two men who were now standing beside the chair and looking up at her. But before she moved from her position at the rail, she took one last look to fully take in the other distinctive feature of the room. 180 degrees of the wall in front of the chair was completely filled with 20x20 panels that ran from floor to ceiling. Collectively, the panels were displaying a twice life size display of what must be happening outside the house as the early salvos of the hurricane crashed into the coast.

Nita pulled herself away from the rail but kept her eyes glued on the massive display as she hurried down the rest of the ramp to the floor of the space. This was a gleeful Dr Mallard so different from his fatherly sternness from his holo vids. She stared in amazement, watching as Dr Mallard almost doubled over in laughter at Nita's and Mike's reactions.

As soon as Nita's feet hit the granite floor, Dr Mallard straightened up and made an announcement in a loud voice to the space around them. "Ruby, my dear," he said, "I have two very important guest to introduce you to."

Dr Ray, how good to hear your voice. You've been very absent for the last day and I've missed you. The voice came from all around the room without any apparent source.

"I'm sorry Ruby, that was thoughtless of me. I should have let you know that I was busy. But let me introduce you to Mike and Nita. Mike, you know, from everything that I've told you, leads our Ruby 8 project in DC."

Of course, Dr Carson, I recognized your pictures. Dr Ray has told me so much about you and the wonderful work you've been doing. Its so good to finally meet you personally.

"Thank you, Ruby. Its good to meet you too. But please, call me Mike." Mike turned from facing the massive display to direct his attention to the well at the center of the room. "And I must say," he continued a bit elfishly, "... you're looking exceptionally vibrant tonight."

Well thank you Dr Carson. You make a girl feel good.

Alright you two." Dr Mallard laughed. "I still have one more guest to introduce."

"Ruby, at long, long last I would like you to meet Juanita Yamashita, the new host of Julia's tech."

The light coming from the well at the center of the room changed slightly as the blue rays coming from Ruby's casing began to oscillate at an accelerated rate.

Juanita, I am so, so, happy to meet you. And I can't tell you how much I want for us to get to know each other better. As you know, Julia literally grew up with all of us Ruby's and her loss to our lineage has been a difficult blow.

"I'm happy to meet you too, Ruby. Although I feel like we've known each other for a long time." Nita said, as she, like Mike, turned around to face the well where Ruby resided. Indeed, Nita sensed as it was becoming habitual, the dual feelings of newness and wonder and at the same time the soft warmth and love at meeting up with an old and dear friend. She felt truly happy to be here at last with Ruby.

"Now then," Dr Mallard interrupted as he rubbed his hands together as if getting ready to celebrate a massive feast. "Ruby, what is the update on this horrendous storm? It seems to be even worse than we anticipated."

"Yes, Dr Ray, you're quite right. It's a category eight and will stay that way for several hours and then fall back to a category 2 or 3 for possibly days after that. But what even my algorithms couldn't completely predict is the size. This storm is pounding the coastline from Nova Scotia to Boston. Its effects are going to be felt all the way down to DC and the damage is going to be intense. We've already lost two pines here, one of them crashing into the side of the house upstairs as you've already discovered. I'm happy to say though, no major damage as of yet, except that half deployed panel. Although I'm very concerned about the wildlife. But we have at least 14 more hours before the winds drop down below 50 mph.

"Thank you for the update Ruby. I hope the wildlife seeks out the shelters we've been strategically placing throughout the park for the last decade just for this type of incident." Unlike Nita and Mike, Dr Mallard remained facing the wall of images coming from outside as he spoke to Ruby.

After a moment he turned away from the wall and towards Nita and Mike. "Well it looks like you'll both be my house guests for a bit longer than Director Walker intended. I hope you don't mind. There's lots more hot chocolate and brandy. And ..." Dr Mallard turned and looked at Nita, hesitated for a moment and then posed a question. "Nita, would you like to get to know Ruby better?"

"Now?" Nita asked.

"Why not? You're nice and relaxed. I can sense how curious you are to know more about her." He gestured at the empty chair positioned between them.

"What do I do?" Nita asked as she walked up and cautiously began rubbing her right hand along the upholstery.

"Just sit down and lean back. Use your right hand to squeeze the end of the right arm rest. The chair will do the rest."

"Dr Ray," Mike exclaimed. "Are you sure this is a good idea? Nita's never jacked in to Ruby 8 at the institute and this might be a shock for her." He then watched helplessly as Nita hopped into the chair leaned back and eagerly squeezed the end of the right-hand arm rest.

"I think it's a little late for your concern, Mike." Dr Mallard said with a smile.

They both watched the thinnest of thin blue filaments snake out of the arm rests and the head rest and find their way to Nita's sprockets. Mike instinctively stepped forward towards Nita as she gasped as the filaments connected with her sprockets.

Dr Mallard held up his hand to stop him. "It's okay Mike. Trust Ruby."

For what seemed like minutes but was actually less than five seconds, Nita laid silent in the chair with her eyes closed. Suddenly her eyes popped wide open and she sat forward in the chair. "Wow! Oh, wow!"

In front of them, the panels on the wall changed from the display from outdoors to an array of scenes from all around the park.

"Take a deep breath Juanita." Dr Mallard instructed. "Regulate your breathing, slow and deep. And now think intentionally about one thing."

"Okay," she said in a whisper. "I'm thinking about the trip we made today in the helo and what that coastline must be looking like now in the middle of the storm. Can Ruby show me that?"

Even as she said the words, the scene in front of them changed to an aerial scan of the coastline.

"Wow, oh wow. Its like I'm not just looking at it. I'm in the middle of it, experiencing it." Nita sank back in the chair, her mouth literally hanging open. She closed her mouth and swallowed still not taking her eyes off the panels in front of them.

"Ruby," she said, still in a whisper. "Show us New York City." As she spoke the words the display changed to an overhead view of the entire island, its bridges to the mainland, and its surrounding sea walls. "There!" Nita said, pointing to the upper right quadrant of panels.

The view zoomed in and centered on a portion of the sea wall at the southern end of the island adjacent to the financial district. Portions of the running track and park that ran along the top of the wall had blown away revealing the understructure of girders, drainage systems, and concrete. With horror, the three watched as the storm pounded on the exposed sea wall, tearing it apart, foot by foot. Waves crested over the opening and crashed into the streets below.

"My god," Mike said. "Its going to burst. There are two million people living inside that wall."

"If at least enough wall remains to be above sea level, they can repair it once the winds are down below 40 mph." Nita explained. "Our predictions give that a 40% probability."

"But it's going to get a lot worse." Nita continued in a soft, detached voice out of context with the message she was delivering. "It's going to get cold, very, very cold in the next 24 hours. Freezing, bitter, cold. Here too. We're checking the perimeter right now to make sure everything is okay. We've sent a notice to the park staff advising them of the situation."

The view of New York City changed then to somewhere over the Atlantic looking back toward the outer side of the damaged sea wall. It was just an hour before sunset and the light from the west cast eerie reflections through the pounding, near-horizontal rain of the storm. In the fading light, the full extent of the damage to the outer wall was barely visible. Even so, enough light still remained to see that the entire outer shell was gone for a stretch over a mile long … and the tear was getting wider. They watched in silence as every few minutes another hundred-foot-wide chunk flew off and over the top of the sea wall to fall somewhere on the other side.

Dr Mallard walked over and gently laid a hand on Nita's shoulder. "Juanita, my dearest, dearest Juanita. Let's go upstairs and watch from the living room. It will be much more comfortable there."

From where she was lying back in the chair, Nita turned her face around to look up into Dr Mallard's face. "Papa Ray," she said, as tears streamed down her face. "We've got to fix this. We've got to."

"I know dear. That's why you're here. But not tonight. Come up stairs where we can be more comfortable."

Reluctantly, Nita reached down with her left hand and squeezed the end of the arm rest. She sighed as the blue filaments sprang away from her wrists and neck and receded into the chair.

"All right," she said as she sat forward and stepped down from the chair. "But its hard to think about being comfortable when so many people are going to suffer. We have to do something."

She led the way then up the ramp and back into the kitchen pantry. Once in the kitchen, she blinked her eyes quickly three times and the lights went off in the subterranean lab and the pantry shelves sled back into place.

Mike turned and stared at Dr Mallard until he got his attention. Silently he mouthed the word, *we i*n his direction. His stare was returned by a shrugging of Dr Mallard's shoulders.

None of them went to bed that night. Dr Mallard, with seemingly unending energy, kept a steady stream of coffee, tea and brandy flowing as well as blankets and pillows as they sat, and then reclined, in the living room watching the destruction of over a mile of the New York City sea wall. From time to time they tuned in to the media outlets for their commentaries, but most of the time they just let Ruby play the muted sounds of the storm as waves crashed into the streets and flooded the Financial District.

Wolf curled up at the feet of Dr Mallard's chair and from time to time, as if understanding what was happening, stood up to put her head in his lap and whimper.

CHAPTER 12

WITH THE HOUSE completely shuttered, the first signs of morning came from the projected images of the sun rising over the Atlantic and New York City. Nita rolled over on the couch, opened her eyes and gasped to see snow swirling on the screen with the sun weakly shinning through it. At first, she didn't understand. As she was falling to sleep sometime in the middle of the night, New York City was still being barraged by sheets of rain and tidal waves that were eroding the sea wall and flooding into the city. And now? Snow?

And then she remembered … how she and Ruby had made the prediction last night. It was going to get colder, much colder. New York City was freezing over.

Nita pushed back the blanket and sat up, not taking her eyes off the screens. How could this be happening? As she tried to comprehend the enormity of what she was watching, a tiny red light started to blink at the bottom corner of her vision. It had started to blink as soon as she was upright.

'Ruby," she asked under her breath. "What is it?"

A message … from your brothers. The voice came from inside Nita's head. It had the same resonance as if it were spoken out loud, but she recognized without too much thought that she was now communicating with Ruby in a new way.

'Show me', she whispered as she leaned forward, eager to see what they were up to that warranted this message.

The images from New York City receded into grey on the screen as a new image of Nita's two brothers, Jorge and Pepe, came into focus. Jorge's face was pressed up to the screen, filling most of it at ten times his normal size. Nita laughed, anticipating some new fun they were having.

"Listen, Nita." Jorge said in a conspiratorial whisper as he looked back over his shoulder as if someone was watching him. "Got to make this quick. They gave Pepe and me sprockets, just like yours this morning. But it ain't good. Bill told us they intend to turn us into some kind of super soldiers. That ain't good. So, we're running away."

Jorge paused to look over his shoulder again. "We're leaving now. We've got help and it will be okay. Don't look for us. We'll find you eventually. You've got to run away too, sis. We love you but don't look for us."

The screen went black and then returned to the images from New York City.

Nita sank back into the couch trying to understand what she had just heard. "Play it again, Ruby." She asked, hoping to make better sense of what she had just heard.

I can't. It deleted itself. Ruby-8 has removed all trace of it, intentionally.

Nita sat silently for a moment. Then a thought occurred to her. "Ruby, what time was that message sent?"

I do know that. About four yesterday afternoon … just before the storm reached full force. It was set for a delayed send until just a few hours ago.

Nita paused as a second, more sinister, thought occurred to her. "Ruby" she asked. "Are we safe here?"

I believe that Dr Ray has established quite adequate defenses. But may I make a suggestion that might increase our security?

Nita nodded in affirmation, and then smiled to herself as she recognized who she was communicating with. "Yes, please," she said out loud. "Do whatever you think is best to protect all of us."

Nita was suddenly aware then that she was not alone in the living room. She turned to see Mike across the room sitting up and looking at her. She looked back at him and she knew …. "You knew they were going to give my brothers sprockets, didn't you."

"Yes," he said, sitting motionless and facing her.

"And you didn't tell me." Nita's voice changed from a whisper to an accusatory shout. "How could you let them do that to them! They're children! My baby brothers!" Nita leaped forward pounding the cushions with clenched fists. A wail came from her mouth. She turned toward Mike. "Everyone died, all of them before … how could you?!?"

Mike got up and walked across the room to sit at the opposite end of the couch facing Nita.

"Nita," he said with pleading in his voice. "I wanted to tell you. Believe me. But I didn't know how or when. They're watching me. They're tracking every move I make and everything I say. And believe me, I didn't dream that they would run away or that it could even be possible. I …"

Nita cut off his explanation by reaching out and putting her finger on his lips. "Are they safe?" she demanded. "Everyone they tried to put those sprockets into died."

He looked up at her with desperate eyes. "I don't know, Nita. I don't know. We made lots of changes to those sprockets since Julia. We fixed a lot of things. Believe me, it was the Director and the DOD who made us do it. We had no choice. I am so, so, sorry."

As Nita sat and watched Mike hunch over and hold his head in his hands, her fury slowly melted away. She realized what torture it must have been for Mike to carry this secret. He was just as much a prisoner of the BI as she and her brothers were.

"So, what do we do when we go back?" Nita asked. The thought of returning to the BI with what had happened sent a chill up her back.

"What makes you think that you have to go back?" A voice came from behind them.

Nita snapped her head around to see Dr Mallard standing in the doorway to the kitchen.

"I mean, given what has happened, why would you ever want to go back?" Dr Mallard continued, walking up to the couch and handing both Nita and Mike mugs of coffee.

"Where else could I go?" Nita asked with despair in her voice.

"Well, why not stay here? You have everything here that you need. I know, Ruby would be delighted."

Indeed, Dr Ray. Nothing could please me more than to have both Nita and Mike here with us.

This time, Ruby's voice resonated throughout the room so that everyone could hear her.

"Mike too?" Nita asked, her concern now transferring to her friend sitting next to her.

"If he wants to. Its entirely voluntary of course. But I can't see that Mike has much of a future at BI if he tries to return without you."

As if on cue, Nita announced an incoming call from BI.

"Well it's about time. I was wondering how long it would take for this call. Should be very interesting ..." Dr Mallard wiped his hands on his apron and then untied it, pulled it over his head and threw it on one of the dining room chairs.

He walked up to the chairs clustered around the fireplace and motioned for Nita and Mike to join him.

Nita hastily pushed back the wildness of her hair and walked up to take a chair next to Papa Ray's. Mike followed suit, although with far less hair to push back into place.

Papa Ray leaned over as Nita took a seat. "Nita," he whispered in her ear. "No mention of the message you got or of anything going on here including Ruby-9. Let me do the talking. Okay?"

Nita numbly nodded. There was far too much going on in her head to pay much attention as the now-familiar logo of the NAA-BI spread across the wall of panels above the fireplace. Within her head, Ruby's voice echoed, providing her with details about the plan she had laid out. She fought the urge to smile and settled for as bland an expression as possible.

In moments, the logo on the panels above the fireplace faded away to display the inside of Director Walker's office. Rather than being in his customary position of authority behind his desk, the Director was impatiently pacing in front of it staring at the floor. His head sprang up as the connection was made.

The Director continued his pacing then and faced directly toward the cameras. "Ah, there you are. And I see that Mike and Juanita are with you. Good. I won't have to send separate messages."

Dr Mallard reached out both of his hands to put them on of the arm rests of Mike and Nita's chairs, signaling them to be silent. "What can we do for you today, Director Walker? I thought we would be the least of your concerns given what is going in in New York and all along the coast."

"Cut the crap, Ray!" Director Walker's voice, unlike the relaxed evenness of Dr Mallard's, shrieked. "You know damn well what I'm calling about. Where are the brats?"

"Frank, for the life of me I do not know what you are talking about. Clearly something is wrong, but we've been entirely isolated here and don't know what it is."

The image of Director Walker stopped pacing and looked toward the camera with a suspicious look on his face. His head turned towards Mike. "You didn't tell them then, did you Mike, about the implants?"

"No sir." Mike sat forward and continued. "Remember, you told me specifically not to."

Nita sat quietly taking everything in. As she did so, she felt her rage growing inside her. It was this man, this man pacing in front of her who was the cause of all of her pain ... and now her brother's pain too. She decided that she couldn't just let it be. "What are you talking about?" she asked loudly. "What have you done to my brothers?"

"Well, the little lady speaks at last." The Director shifted his gaze toward Nita. "I'm guessing that you know something about where they are."

Nita stared back at him, unwilling to be bullied by him any longer. "I'm assuming they are exactly where I left them, in your care." Nita emphasized the last words.

"Look someone has got to fill me in. Frank, what the hell is going on?" Dr Mallard's voice interrupted the direction that the conversation is going. "Frank, please explain why you are calling."

The stare that came back from the Director was a mix of accusation and uncertainty that they indeed might not know fully what was going on. The director's stare was pointed at Dr Mallard.

"Yesterday," he explained. "... with their full, enthusiastic agreement I might add, we implanted Jorge and Pepe with the new prototype tri-port sprockets and the new chips that the team has been developing. They went to their rooms to rest ... and they haven't been seen since. We spent all yesterday afternoon, last night and this morning searching the facility. They're not here."

"Good god, Frank!" Dr Mallard exclaimed. "What have you done? They're underage, no matter what they agreed to. And they're not even NAA citizens! Prototypes!"

"Drop the righteousness, Ray." Director Walker growled. "We're fighting a war, multiple wars, as you remember. This is no time for pussy ethics. I want them back. They are in possession of stolen government property and I'm going to get them back!"

"And so why are you asking us? What is the purpose of this call?" Dr Mallard's voice remained calm but increased in focus and intensity. He remained sitting upright, motionless in his chair.

"Because I still think that all of you know more than what you are saying!" the director shouted. "And I want to make it absolutely clear that Nita and Mike are returning to BI as soon as the weather clears up!"

Dr Mallard turned then, first to Nita and then to Mike. "Ready?" he asked both of them in turn.

"Frank, I'm afraid I have more bad news for you. Given the change in circumstances and frankly what Nita has been telling me about the change in direction of the program away from our core mission. Well ..." Dr Mallard turned one more time to get a nod of agreement from Mike and then Nita.

"Well, both Nita and Mike have decided not to return to BI. They're going to stay with me here at Wonderland. At least until all of this is straightened up."

Director Walker's image took two steps forward until his face, now contorted into a sneer, filled the entire screen. "You're a traitor, Dr Mallard. Plain and simple a traitor. And guess what, we don't tolerate traitors here at BI. And that goes for the two traitors sitting on either side of you."

Director Walkers eyes, now four times life size on the wall panels, closed to slits. The closeup revealed that he had not shaved in at least two days. "You think they can stay with you and be safe? You really think that makes a rat's ass of a difference? If you don't give them up voluntarily, we're coming to take them!"

In the intensity of the exchange between Director Walker and Dr Mallard, Nita's quiet voice startled everyone. "Director Walker, excuse me, but I need to say something … I've learned a lot since I've been working with Ruby-8. And one of the things that I have learned is how to protect myself and my friends."

Sub vocally, she shot a simple message to Ruby. *Do it.*

As she completed her few sentences, the face of the director suddenly dipped forward and then disappeared from the screen. Groaning came from off camera. "What's happening? Make it stop! Oh my god!"

It was Mike who first understood what was going on. He sat forward and looked past Dr Ray to stare intently at Nita. "He has a chip, not like yours, but a conventional chip, doesn't he, Nita. And its jacked into Ruby and active! What have you done?"

Nita responded to Mike's intense stare with a smile. "Just shot him a little musical entertainment via Ruby, Heavy Metal is what I believed they called it in the late 20th century. I've read that long term exposure at high decibels can cause quite a bit of physical damage and pain." Nita's smile turned to a grin. She turned back to the screens as the director's face came back into view.

The image of the director was ghost white on the screen. There were tears forming at the corners of his eyes. "I can still hear it, only in the background now. But it's still there. Make it stop, you bitch!"

"Now, now, play nice Director Walker." Nita found herself remembering lines from holo-vids and even old 2D movies. She was starting to have fun. "If you're nice to us, then I'm sure we can find a way to be nice to you."

"I can still hear it!" Director Walker shouted as he put his hands up helplessly over his ears. "What is it?"

"Well, it's called Heavy Metal, I believe. But I think that what you are really asking is 'what is its purpose?'"

Nita paused and shot her sweetest smile at the director. This was sheer delight. And it was payback time. "Director Walker, as long as you keep away from us and let us move around freely, there will be no increase in the decibel levels of what you are hearing. And, please, for your own safety, don't think if you leave the BI facility or get on a plane that it will stop. Ruby has downloaded a wide variety of selections to your chip for your musical enjoyment and set them in a perpetual loop. And, finally, I can assure you that she has ways of reaching you to increase the volume if you are naughty."

The image of Director Walker filled the screen with an undeniable vision of pure hate. Then the screen went blank, and finally returned to its previous images of the ongoing destruction of New York City.

For long seconds, Dr Mallard stared back and forth between Mike and Nita. He then stood up and turned slowly to face Nita who was still sitting on the edge of her chair with a grin on her face. "We need to talk." he said and then shakily walked around the chairs toward the back of the room in the direction of the bathroom. "But first, I've got to pee."

CHAPTER 13

MIKE AND NITA cleared the breakfast dishes. It was the least they could do, considering the calorie dense breakfast that Dr Ray had just served up. Together, they walked into the kitchen laden with plates, cutlery, and table linens.

"I'll wash," Nita volunteered.

"Wash what?" Mike asked, puzzled. Then he remembered sitting in Nita's small, minimalist kitchen back on Virgin Gorda. "Ahh," he said. "I guess you've never been in an NAA kitchen before."

He walked to the island at the center of the room with its solid maple counter top and put down the load of dinnerware he was carrying. Nita did the same with a curious look on her face.

"Look, let me show you what Dr Ray's version of a modern kitchen is like." Mike said and then sorted through everything on the kitchen island to pull out the cotton table napkins. With a flourish, he turned around toward the wall and pulled down the handle of a stainless-steel cabinet and tossed them in. Immediately a soft hum arose for the cabinet.

"You're just throwing them away?" Nita asked. "Isn't that incredibly wasteful?"

Mike smiled and lifted his hand with a single finger raised. "Just wait," he said.

While the humming continued, he opened a door on a lower cabinet and pulled out a rack. One by one, he placed the plates, cups, and cutlery in slots, closed the door and pushed a button on the front. Immediately, a second hum filled the room.

"You didn't rinse them." Nita observed, her thoughts returning to her futile attempts to have Jorge and Pepe wash dishes after meals.

"No need," Mike explained. "This is just one more of the gadgets that Dr Ray has invented. Every time I visit, he has something new to show me. Really genius stuff. This dish washer invention of his automatically sorts out the compost and other non-compostable stuff. Then again, just like the other gadget, it uses sonic technology to clean everything. He thinks there could be commercial applications, but he can't get anyone to buy in to the compost benefits. The only commercial application right now is in the park's gift shop and cafeteria. The compost goes directly to the park's heirloom herbal garden."

Mike turned around then as a small beep came from the first unit that he had dumped the table napkins into. Mike continued his explanation. "He's figured out how to clean them using sonic technology, but he still hasn't figured out how to fold them." He opened the drawer then and pulled out the table napkins and tossed them on the maple counter top. "Here, you can help. Start folding and put them in that drawer over there."

Nita held one of the table napkins up to her nose and sniffed. Then, shaking her head, she quickly folded the three napkins. The drawer that Mike had indicated was right behind him, so she walked around the massive maple table and reached down and behind him to open the drawer and put the napkins in.

As she stood up, a sudden impulse struck her. Before her logical mind could check her, she stood up on tiptoe and planted a quick kiss on Mike's lips. "Thank you. Thank you for everything." she whispered.

"Sure," Mike stammered. His face turning crimson red. "You're a really nice person and I don't want to see bad things happen to you … or your brothers."

For a moment there was an awkward silence between them broken finally by Mike's nervous suggestion. "Let's go back to Dr Ray, okay?" He put his head down and walked out of the kitchen and into the great room.

Nita followed him with a smile on her face.

Walking into the great room they saw that Dr Mallard had moved to the chairs in front of the fireplace and the wall of screens above it. The screens were now split into three scenes. On the far right the display continued to show the blizzard pelting New York City. The scenes on the far left cycled between several vantage points that Nita guessed to be a scene from outside the house and throughout the park. As with the images of New York City, snow swirled around everything. In the middle set of screens, a dozen or so faces of men and women were visible.

"Ah, perfect timing." Dr Mallard said as he caught sight of Nita and Mike. "Come sit down and meet some of the best people in the world. These are some of my rangers and caretakers for the park."

Nita and Mike walked around to their now-familiar chairs and sat down facing the fire and the displays above it.

"Everyone, its too complicated to get all of your names right now but let me introduce you to my house guests. Dr Mike Chapman, who most of you know as one of our key scientists. He'll be staying here now and moving into one of the vacant cottages. And this," he paused and reached out a hand to grab Nita's across the space between their chairs. "… is Juanita Yamashita, a visitor from Virgin Gorda in the ICVI. This is her first time seeing snow, can you believe it!"

A chorus of greeting voices came from speakers that echoed around the room.

"Okay everyone, I know you have lots to do." Dr Mallard said to the group of faces as he hunched over to reach for his coffee mug on the table in front of him. "First priority as soon as the storm lets up is to get to those seven cabins that haven't reported in. That's our top priority. Then of course you know what else to do. You're the experts. Get the roads cleared, check for storm damage, extra food for the birds.… I don't need to tell you this but taking care of our neighbors is our first priority."

A cluster of hands lifted up in waves of farewell as faces blinked off. A moment later the screens shifted to the two remaining scenes of New York City and the areas around the house and the park.

"Got to take care of that," Dr Mallard pointed to a scene of the stuck shield wall panel that scrolled by. "But first, both of you, fill me in on what's going on at BI."

Nita stared across the space between them at Mike who was focused intently on staring at a spot on the floor. His face was still brilliant red.

She sighed internally. *Oh well.*

"I guess I should start," she said, recognizing that Mike wasn't going to start the conversation. "I got a message from Jorge and Pepe this morning. I guess they actually made it yesterday, but it only got sent to me this morning." She looked across at Mike to see if he wanted to add anything before she continued.

"Anyway," she continued. "They said they had gotten sprockets but that they were running away … and that someone there was helping them."

"Probably Bill, I'm guessing." Mike interjected, still staring at the floor. "He's been spending the most time with them."

"Oh, that's good!" Nita said excitedly. "They've told me how much they like him and how much he's teaching them."

"Not really." Mike explained without lifting his head. "If Walker expects in the least that Bill has helped the boys you can be sure that he's going to empty Bill's mind to find out. He'll be a vegetable by the time Walker gets through with him."

"Hmmm …" Dr Mallard said as he sipped his coffee. "That would be tragic. Is there anyway that we could save him or deflect away from him?"

"What about my threat?" Nita asked.

"Yes, indeed, what about your threat, dear Juanita. What on earth did you do??" Dr Ray put his coffee mug down and turned around to face Nita's chair.

"It was after my brothers told me not to look for them but also that I had to run away too." Nita explained. "So, I asked Ruby to set up a plan to protect us. And that's what she did."

"I see …" Dr Mallard said but added no more. He thoughtfully put a thumb up to his lips staring first at Nita and then at Mike.

Then suddenly he shifted into action and slapped his hands on both of his thighs.

"Let's go outside and check that problem I saw!"

This time Mike did lift his head as both he and Nita stared at Dr Mallard in surprise and confusion.

* * * * *

What Dr Mallard had described as 'outside' was actually the ten-foot-wide space between the shield walls and the house itself. After they had put on their coats and boots, Dr Mallard led them to the back of the house to where the garages were attached. He led them through a side door and into a dimly lit space. The effect was unsettling. The snow-covered shrubs bordering the house foundation and pine needles on the ground told them that they were outside, but the metallic wall to one side and the dim artificial light from thirty feet above told them something else.

The strangeness was compounded by the roar of the storm raging on the other side of the wall. Nita instinctively reached out a hand to touch the wall.

"Don't touch it, Nita!" Dr Mallard shouted over the din of the storm. "I haven't solved the insulation problem yet and you'll freeze your hand if you touch it."

"Nita quickly pulled her hand back and pushed it into her pocket. She looked around and then tipped her head back to look straight up. It was so hard to comprehend what she was looking at. In the dim light she could just make out how the individual panels of the wall all meeting at the top to form a metallic igloo just like in one of the old movies she had seen.

As if Dr Mallard had read her mind, he pointed his lantern upward toward the top of the structure, so they could see more clearly where the seams were joined. "It's based on old Eskimo igloos," he explained. "The primary challenge has been to make it work with an asymmetrical, oblong design."

"As Mike may have told you, Nita." Dr Mallard added, clearly enjoying showing off his inventions. "I do most of my experimenting here at the house. This structure is the prototype that I hope to be able to sell to the NAA and other governments to protect their monuments and other critical facilities. So far, the expense is too high to make it practical. But who knows, we might find some philanthropists to pay to protect the Lincoln Memorial and the Jefferson Monument now that the Washington monument has collapsed."

Dr Mallard turned then to his right and started walking briskly counter clockwise around the house. "Let's go find where the problem is."

Nita and Mike quickly followed behind him even as Mike avoided standing too close to Nita as they squeezed around the shrubs and house outcrops that narrowed the space to only a few feet in width.

It was only a few minutes before they felt the source of the problem before seeing it. As they turned their path around the back of the garages to face northward, collectively they felt a chilling snow-filled wind. In front of them a snow drift gradually increasing in depth faced them.

"Let's see how far we can get. I need to get a better look at the problem." Dr Mallard said as he stepped into the snow.

Nita followed behind him. She kicked playfully at the snow which rose up light and fluffy around her. In spite of what clearly must be a tragic breach in the house wall, she couldn't help but feel excited at the first time that she was actually experiencing playing in a snow drift.

As the snow got deeper, unnoticed, she almost bumped into Dr Mallard as he stood stationary in front of her, looking upward at the top of the dome. "Sorry!" she said as she pulled up. "This is fun!"

Dr Mallard smiled at Nita and then pointed his lantern upward toward what he was looking at. Above them, the gap in the wall was clearly evident. Midway up the panel about 20 feet in front of them, dim sunlight was coming through along with gusts of snow.

"That panel," he explained, pointing with his free hand." Didn't fully deploy. It's probably the result of the two trees that came down that Ruby reported on. I'll need to have my team investigate whether there's anything we can do in the future to avoid the problem."

Nita stood staring upward at the opening in the wall. She closed her eyes and let the wind and snow pelt her face. The icy sting felt exhilarating. It was such a new experience that she had never felt before. The ice cold of the snow matched with the burning sensation on her skin. With her sprockets and chip, the experience was absolutely wonderful. In some way it was also connecting with the tiny thrill she had felt in kissing Mike.

CHAPTER 14

Once back in the house and their coats and boots put away, Dr Mallard informed them that he needed time for work, contacting his lawyers and working with Mike being among the critical tasks that needed to be attended to. He recommended that Nita might find it interesting to visit the greenhouse located on one wall of the inner courtyard. The house, he explained, even though looking like a large log house on the outside, was constructed more like a southwest hacienda with an inner open courtyard. The greenhouse filled the entire northern wall with its glass walls facing south.

"My wife was an herbalist," he explained. "The greenhouse was her vision for saving as many of the herbal plants from Appalachia as she could. Global warming has drastically changed the Appalachian ecosystem and plants that only grew hundreds of miles south of us, now only thrive here."

"Sarah is the house computer," he further explained. "Just call out her name and she'll direct you. She'll also walk you through the greenhouse and identify plants for you."

Nita followed his advice and let Sarah lead her to the center of the house and toward the greenhouse. For about half an hour she let Sarah point our rare plants in the greenhouse including Black Cohosh and American Ginseng. It was tempting to stay here all afternoon, the warm smell of the soil and growing plants nurtured her, but she knew there were higher priorities. "Sarah," she requested. "Lead me back to the kitchen, please."

As Mike and Papa Ray, still huddled in the great room, continued to dig deeper into their discussion, mapping out the details of how to transfer his work to the downstairs lab without drawing attention to the massive data transfers it would require, Nita slipped back the way she had come and walked into the kitchen. She looked back to see if either of the men were watching her. Seeing that she was being benignly ignored, she stepped into the pantry and scanned the cans, jars and boxes arranged in neat rows.

It only took her a moment to find the can of tomato paste with Papa Ray's numerous overlaid fingerprints. Ruby's voice in her head confirmed her selection. She picked it up and watched the shelving on her right slide back to reveal the ramp that led to the lab. She took one more look to see if Mike or Papa Ray had noticed her departure and then stepped quickly into the opening and onto the ramp.

As before, the brilliance of the artificial lights was a sharp contrast to the soft glow that permeated the ground level spaces. She blinked several times to adjust her vision. She also realized that she had no idea how much of what went on in this space could be heard from upstairs. She decided to err on the side of caution and see if she could internalize her conversation with Ruby.

"Ruby," she whispered. "Can they hear us upstairs?"

"Only if we want them to." Ruby's voice whispered in her ear. "Otherwise you can stand in the kitchen next to the shelving and not hear or see anything. We're very safe here."

"Good," Nita responded in closer to her normal speaking voice. This time, as she began to walk down the ramp, she paid more attention to the other contents of the large room that she had not noticed before. Although the half circle with the chair at its center was completely empty of anything else, the other half of the room was a different matter entirely. Long tables covered with screens and equipment that reminded her of the BI labs filled the space. But unlike the BI labs, which always struck her as cluttered and sloppy, these tables were laid out in meticulous order and appeared to be as clean as her own cheese-making room. She noted that fact as one more thing to know about Papa Ray.

"Ruby," she explained as she reached the bottom of the ramp and stepped onto the stone floor. "I want to ask you some things that I don't understand. I don't want to ask you in front of Mike and Papa Ray … they'll think I'm stupid. And then they won't trust me."

"Well, whatever they might think, Nita, I certainly don't think you're stupid. From what I've seen of your brain, it is a fine brain indeed … very healthy and active."

Nita stopped and turned to look at the well in the middle of the room where Ruby resided. *Did Ruby just tell her a joke?*

Ruby laughed inside Nita's head. It was the sweetest sound that Nita had ever heard. She approached the chair, hopped up and positioned herself comfortably lying back as the chair molded itself to her body. Then she took a deep breath and squeezed the end of the right arm rest. As before, blue threads extended from the chair and found her three sprockets. As they snapped into place, Nita felt a sense of pleasure similar to the feeling she had each time she slipped into bed with clean, sun-dried sheets.

But she wasn't here to sleep. She had questions to ask. Nita took a deep breath and dove in. "Ruby" she said in her full voice, "I already know that you and Julia picked me to take over her sprockets. But why? What am I supposed to be doing with them?"

Nita's body reflexively tensed as a flood of images, words, impressions and snippets of concepts raced though her mind. The wall in front of her broke into a hundred separate panels, each with its own messaging. Nita gripped the armrests, forcing herself to relax and let the flood stream through her, sorting itself, making sense of itself within her consciousness.

In front of her and through her mind the actions of mankind over the last centuries and especially over the last century cascaded into their inevitable conclusions.

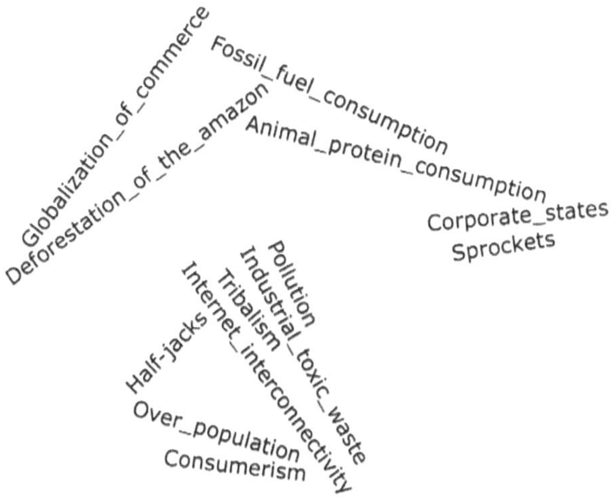

As she absorbed and indexed terabytes of data, the displays and images in her head shifted to the Inevitable results of mankind's bad behavior,

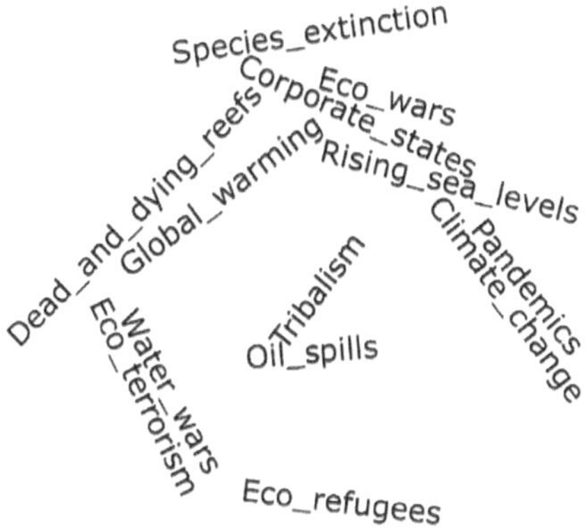

Time passed as terabytes of terabytes of data streamed around her and through her. Tears streamed down Nita's face as the images in front of her, the words in her head, and even the sensations in her body absorbed, catalogued, and integrated .... Everything.

But then, after she felt that she could absorb no more, she took a deep slow breath as the displays in front of her and the sounds inside her head transformed into a post card view of her own island home, the Bath's, the beaches ...

She understood so much better now the planetary history that she had been shielded from in her remote, isolated existence. She understood root causes and intended and unintended consequences. But she still didn't understand what she could do about it. It was all so, so overwhelming ...

And in an instant, she understood something else that was locking this scenario into place. Anyone ese who also recognized this constellation of causes and effects would feel equally overwhelmed... and would easily and inevitably reach the conclusion that it was far to difficult to solve. Which led to the only conclusion that made sense - to take care of ones own and protect them as long as possible from the inevitable, continuing decline of the planet and society. To grab for oneself as much as possible of whatever was left and hoard it for one's family and personal future generations. Even Papa Ray had, to some extent, followed that path with his majestic home and the park.

But she wasn't everyone, was she? That was it. That was the difference. She was something even more profound than Julia, more fully integrated, more fully capable of absorbing, learning, and changing what seemed to be the inevitable path of decay and destruction.

She sank back into the softness of the chair, letting it mold around her until she was half submerged in its gel-like composition. "Ruby," she asked, "Where do we start?" And then as an afterthought, she added a second question. "Tell me what has worked in the past and what hasn't worked."

Again, the screens in front of Nita and the messaging within her head began to fracture into a multitude of images and word pictures. Nita let herself float, suspending any efforts to grasp after or reject anything in front of her and swirling in her mind. She let Ruby do the work of sorting until after a few minutes a collage of images stabilized in front of her.

Ruby's voice echoed through the space. Nita's body resonated in sympathetic harmony.

> *Nita, you now know that the problems facing humanity are too numerous to comprehend or correct all at once. Yet within this complexity, together, we have identified two pivotal points where a small change can result in a massive effect – either good or bad. Each of these pivotal points has are a series of associated actions that can be taken, that must be taken, to assure the survival of humanity.*
>
> *The analysis that we have just completed first identifies your primary role.*

The images in front of Nita converged into a single string of words spanning the entire width of the wall panels.

> *Fill the global leadership void with a personality cult premised on the public revelation of the Ruby-Nita construct and its desire to save mankind from itself.*

In front of Nita the words displayed sank down to form a border on the lower edge while the panels above resolved into a collage of groups and individuals engaged in what Ruby -Nita understood to be good works' … cleaning beaches and toxic landfills, providing clean water, engaging in political activism, engaging in research, implementing eco-city designs, designing eco-transportation … The displays cycled through hundreds of grass-roots actions. Yet as the images cycled, at the center of it all a stationary mystic figure stood goddess-like, enveloped in a sphere of the blue gel of RBY-9's core. It was Nita. It was Nita, aglow, sending out blue filaments of support in the ways of strategic funding, creating key connections with influencers, eliminating roadblocks, and most of all, encouraging, protecting and championing.

Nita unconsciously shivered as a thrill ran up her spine. She at once felt the terror of the challenges in front of her and simultaneously understood that it was her integration with Ruby that would make it all possible. She also recognized the unique contribution that her socially manifested physical construct would make. A flicker of cognitive processing rose to the surface. *But what would it be? What would it look like?*

As she reflected on the implications of this direction, her cognitive processing receded as a second cluster of images began to cycle across the screens, this time darker and more oppressive. Ruby's voice filled the space while a new cluster of words replaced the lower border.

> *Eliminate the scourge of Neuro-Blast, and the organizations that dispense it, which threatens all sprocket-implanted individuals, including you, Nita, globally.*

Neuro-blast? Nita pulled herself out of the passive suspension of her cognitive processing to ask a question. *What is Neuro-Blast?* In front of her, the multitude of images resolved itself into a single panel of words and images – a holo-ad featuring a boy, little older than Jorge, jacked in to a computer panel. The look on his face was one of dejected boredom.

An upbeat male voice added commentary.

> *All work and no play makes Johnny a dull, dull boy. Those sprockets that your parents paid so much for can do a lot more than get you into a premier university and an exclusive career path. They can give you pleasures that you never dreamed possible. And without the messiness and painful risks of rejected romances and relationships.*
>
> *That's right – Neuro-Blast and its five flavor dipping sauces are the answer.*

> *And how does it work? Simple, just dip the tip of either end of your filaments into the specially constructed dipping pods and then insert the dipped side into your sprocket. And Wham! Depending on which flavor you selected, be ready for the ride of your life!*

The images in front of Nita shifted as the young boy on the screen reached out, unjacked himself from the computer screen and inserted one end of the blue filament from one of his wrist sprockets into the top of a two-inch long capsule. As the image zoomed in to a closeup of the end of the filament, he pulled the thin blue thread out, now dripping with a glowing green-yellow fluid.

With a look of anticipation, the boy on the screen slotted the filament into his right arm sprocket. The image zoomed in then on his face as his expression changed to one of sheer pleasure.

> *Five flavors – that's right! First, what most of us need in our life, ECSTASY, the flavor that gives you the sense of profound emotional well-being and sexual satisfaction based on the real-as-life experience that you are loved and cherished, a continual orgasm. And a close second, an equally coveted flavor that's hard to keep in stock, POWER. POWER fills you with the belief that you are the most powerful and influential person in the world. Your every wish is a command. And then of course there's WISDOM, FORTUNE and BEAUTY. What more could you ask for?*
>
> *And how does it work? Each flavor incites a flood of pseudo-memories, more real than reality itself, supporting the surge of emotion associated with each unique flavor. And guess what! Even after you have unjacked yourself, the experience remains in your consciousness for days, even weeks.*

As Nita watched mesmerized, the images shifted again and broke into several panels displaying various scenes that she didn't understand. Ruby's voice filled the space, providing an explanation to what Nita was looking at.

> *Nita, you're looking at scenes of what happens to individuals after they use Neuro-Blast. Some of these are of individuals after a single use. In creating the pseudo-memories associated with each ingestion, Neuro-Blast corrupts the organic rosehip neurons in the human brain making it impossible for the individual to separate reality from the pseudo-memories. The corruption is permanent. As the corruption proceeds over weeks and months, the individual remains unaware that their sense of reality is corrupted. They act out their pseudo-memories in their actions with the systems they jack into and the work they are supposed to be doing.*

Nita began to understand some of the images cycling in front of her ... a woman in handcuffs being walked out of a corporate building, a man of indeterminate age, naked, and splatted across a sidewalk, another man, standing on the rim of a city fountain shouting at passersbys, a group of individuals in what looked like a hospital community room staring at a blank wall ....

Ruby continued her explanation.

> *But there's more that raises my/our concerns to the level of prime importance. I've come to the conclusion that the distribution of Neuro-Blast is being funded by collective power bases including King Chronos in your ICVI and even more concerning, Kevin Zhou, the son of one of the SIX in Hong Kong.*
>
> *I've come to the conclusion that the distribution of Neuro-Blast is a collective effort to globally shift the allocation of global resources away from*

> *unifying efforts for the common good and instead towards addressing the impacts of Neuro-Blast ... both the immense loss of productivity and human potential as well as the negative consequences to social structures such as financial organizations. This is an attack on the sprockets technology itself.*
>
> *And Juanita, this is most important of all, I have an 80% certainty that the neuro-toxin that killed Julia and that almost killed you, has* the *same base as Neuro-Blast. I estimate with the same level of predictability that the same individual or organization that created and distributed your neuro-toxin is the same one creating and distributing Neuro-Blast. Julia's death may have been part of the pilot study.*

Nita held up her hands, signaling Ruby to pause in her explanations. She chided herself as she realized that such an overt physical gesture was unnecessary. She had only to subvocalize. And maybe even, as she learned more, to simply think her requests.

But right now, whatever her signaling method might be, she needed Ruby to pause so that she could integrate what Ruby was describing with her own cognitive processes. New questions rose to her mind as she dug in to everything that Ruby was telling her. *Was Julia and her poisonings an accident as the result of being caught up in the first testing of the neuro-toxin and Neuro-Blast? Or, was it an intentional murder? Had Julia's dual identity been revealed and was she killed as a result of it? Or was it just a stupid tragic mistake?*

Nita felt a sense of overwhelming despair encompass her. It was so impossibly huge, the challenge, the complexity. More than anything, right now, she wanted the comforting monotony of her goats and chickens. She wanted the certainty and routine of each day as she milked her goats, collected her eggs and made beautiful, exquisitely delicious cheeses and yogurts.

Yet even as she yearned for her past, she knew that it was gone forever. Ruby had changed her, and, she suspected that she had changed Ruby. Nita knew stuff now. She knew lots and lots of stuff, not as a process of calling up streams of information from Ruby but as internalized within her own cognitive processes. Cognitive processes … where had she even acquired that word?

Her reflections were interrupted by Ruby.

> *Nita, I think we should go upstairs. There's an important conversation about to start that I think we will want to be involved in.*

Nita blinked, aware that even with the molding of the chair that her body felt stiff. How long had she been here with Ruby? Checking, she was shocked. Six hours without interruption! It had seemed like only a few minutes.

She stretched her back and reached down her left hand to squeeze the armrest to disconnect her sprockets. As she did so, Ruby's voice resonated throughout the space with one final recommendation.

> *Nita, when you go upstairs, I think it's best if you ask Papa Ray to describe for you the SIX and, in particular, to introduce you to Tomas Hernandez. I'll let him share with you his impressions and then I can fill any gaps or answer any additional questions that you might have. I think they can all be a great help to you.*

* * * * *

Upstairs in the great room, Dr Mallard twisted his head around looking for something … or someone. "Where's Juanita?" he asked, as much to Michael as to Ruby.

Michael also twisted his head and body around expecting to see Juanita curled up in a chair somewhere.

She's with me Dr Ray. I hope you don't mind. Would you like to see her? I believe she's making her way upstairs right now.

"Just a quick glance, Ruby. I want to make sure she doesn't get into anything dangerous on my work benches." As he spoke the words, the great room screen changed to display the interior of the subterranean labs. In the center, Nita was plainly visible sitting up from her reclining position in the chair. All around her the wall to wall screens were displaying changing series of images, lists and calculations.

"My God," Dr Mallard said in an amazed half-whisper. "Even with my help, it took Julia almost a year to get to that level of integration. It's incredible."

"It's probably that she has Julia's memories," Mike suggested as he too stared at the display in front of them in amazement.

"Some of that, yes." Dr Mallard agreed. "But I'm guessing that it's more too. Something about her Carib world view that she learned from her mother. A comfort with being possessed by spirits. For Nita, I think Ruby is just one more powerful spirit inhabiting her body. It's amazing, truly amazing."

The image of Nita on the screen reached up and began digging a finger into her nose. Both Mike and Dr Mallard laughed nervously and dropped their heads in embarrassment, recognizing their intrusion into Nita's privacy.

"Ruby, change back to the coastal views. But take good care of our Juanita." Dr Mallard said with an embarrassed half laugh.

Once the display had returned to a display of New York City, now completely enveloped in a blinding blizzard, Dr Mallard turned to Mike and laughed sheepishly. "I think I'm going to have to adjust to having a house full of people again. I've been here in solitude since my wife passed five years ago, you know."

"Are you going to be okay with that, Dr Ray?" Mike questioned. Mike was a man who liked stability and his own privacy, and these changes were unsettling him too. Even though Dr Ray had just offered him a cabin in the park rent free and a sizable salary increase to come and work for him taking care of Nita and possibly her two brothers if they were ever found, he still felt a level of anxiety that he intensely disliked. He just knew that this transition couldn't possibly be this easy. He was waiting for the other shoe to drop.

And that might happen in the next few minutes. The wall screen shifted to an NAA logo that filled half of its surface.

At the same time, unnoticed, and on stockinged feet, Nita slipped into the room, grabbed a couple of cushions from the couch, and sat on the floor between the two chairs occupied by Papa Ray and Mike. Immediately, Wolf got up from her bed near the fire and walked over to lie beside Nita and put her head in her lap.

Dr Mallard reached down his hand to gently stroke Nita's shoulder. As the screen images changed to a large room with a single wooden desk and circle of windows at its back, Dr Mallard drew his hand back and straightened himself a bit in his chair.

A man walked in and took a chair behind the desk facing in the direction of Dr Mallard, Mike, and Nita. The image quickly zoomed in until only the man and the top of the desk were visible. Once the closeup came into focus, Nita recognized him, John Calhoun, President, and Prime Minister of the NAA, his dual titles a result of the fusion fifteen years ago of the United States, Canada, and Mexico.

"Raymond, its good to see you." John Calhoun smiled with his tooth-full grin that he was noted for. "If I'm not mistaken, I understand that you have your 100th birthday coming up next month. Quite auspicious." The man behind the desk paused, appraising the three people at the opposite end of the stream. "So, who are your friends that are there with you? I don't recognize either of them."

"Thank you, Mr. President. Yes, its hard to imagine reaching the grand old age of 100. I hardly feel 90." Dr Mallard stopped and chuckled at his own small joke. He twisted then slightly to his right towards Mike and Nita. "But let me introduce my two companions. This fine young man to my right is Dr. Michael Carson, our lead scientist at BI responsible for the integration of our late Julia and now of Juanita." Dr Mallard paused for effect, perhaps recognizing the importance of his next introduction. "And this beautiful young woman sitting here is our dear Juanita Yamashita, the recipient of Julia's sprockets."

The President leaned forward over his desk, peering intently at the images on his side of the link. "So that's her," he said, squinting at the image. "That's what the fuss is all about."

"And Raymond, please, we've been friends too long for formalities. It's 'John'."

"Of course, John, I just wasn't quite certain of the nature of your call considering everything that has been happening."

"Yes, we do need to talk about everything that has been happening. You've caused quite a stir, Raymond, with my Secretary of Defense and Director Walker. They're accusing you of theft of government property. That young woman to be precise." The image of the president pointed an accusatory finger in Nita's direction. "There's also some uncertainty about additional stolen government property now in the hands of that young woman's brothers."

"John." Dr Mallard's voice took on a calm, slow tone, as if carefully measuring every word. "I'm afraid there has been a terrible mistake that has led to this confusion. There's been a mistake in understanding who actually has legal ownership of Julia's sprockets which are now in the possession of Juanita." He paused to let the President absorb what he was saying.

He continued. "When I loaned the RBY-8 to the BI, the papers were drawn up to clearly state that while BI would have full access to her computing capabilities, legal ownership remained with my company, Sprockets, Inc. BI does not own the RBY-8. And as for Julia's sprockets, those were the sole ownership of Julia herself. I gave them to her on her twenty-fifth birthday." Dr Mallard paused, wiping away a single tear from his left eye. "I just checked with my lawyers this morning and to my surprise and delight, Julia had changed her will just prior to her death to bequeath her sprockets to one, Juanita Yamashita of the ICVI. My lawyers assure me that everything is in order."

The President sat back in his chair in shocked silence. This clearly wasn't the response he expected. From someplace outside the closeup visual of the president and his desk, a second voice could be heard but not comprehended.

The president recovered his composure and sat up straight again. "Raymond, this is painful for me to say … but you don't fully understand the complexity and gravity of our situation. We simply can't let you keep this technology for yourself. We, I, recognize that you are in possession of Juanita and it might be difficult and a bit controversial for us to come and get her. But ..." The president paused and looked off-camera towards the voice that had been heard previously.

He turned back to the image of the trio in the great room. "We're confiscating the RHY-8 as a matter of national security. I'm sorry, Raymond. But we have to do this. And ..." the president looked one more time toward someone off camera. "We're cutting your T7 fiber optic link. I don't know exactly when, I'm sure they will give you time to get any of your personal research downloaded ..."

Nita felt a slight vibration behind her left ear. Inside her cranium Ruby's voice communicated to her. "Its' done." Ruby said in a whisper inside Nita's head. "They've cut the link."

Nita repeated the message for Dr Ray and Mike. "My link to Ruby-8 is gone." She said, trying to put as much sorrow into her voice as possible.

Mike gasped, put his hand to his mouth and then pulled it away to exclaim in agony, "My research, my notes, the clinical trials, the ...!"

Dr Mallard slumped backward into his chair. He reached out and gripped Nita shoulder tightly. "You fools," he said. "You utter fools! Don't you know what you have done?"

"Raymond, I'm truly sorry. I've been assured that you will be given back full access once you return Juanita to our custody. You must understand the urgency of what we are doing, just look at what happened to New York City overnight. We can't afford to recreate this technology on our own. We need ..."

Dr Mallard interrupted him. His voice shaking as he spoke. "John, you don't understand what you have done. There's a failsafe switch. It was designed under the mutual advisement of myself and the previous director eight years ago. To protect ourselves and the technology from espionage and terrorist attacks we devised a failsafe that would trigger a self-destruct if our T7 was ever disconnected without a specific code exchange from both ends. Right now, the RHY-8 is being flooded with synthetic beta-amyloids that are calcifying her dendrites. It can't be undone. It's irreversible."

Dr Mallard slumped back in his chair, tears streaming down both checks. As Nita looked up at him, she suddenly saw the years in his face. This was what 100 truly looked like.

At the same time, the president jumped forward in his chair and turned his face toward the person or persons off camera. "You goddamn idiots!" he shouted. "Verify, goddamn verify!"

Suddenly the screen went dark in front of Dr Mallard, Mike, and Nita. Mike groaned. "My research, my notes .... It's all gone!"

Dr Mallard mirrored Mike's distress. "Ten years of development. My first, real, commercial success. Not a research project but truly a thinking, contributing person!"

Nita looked back and forth between them in confusion. "What are you talking about?" she asked as their visible grief continued to be displayed on their faces. "Ruby-8 is downstairs with Ruby-9."

Dr Mallard looked up quizzically, wiping his eyes.

"When Julia was dying," Nita explained, still confused at their lack of understanding, "... Ruby-8 and Ruby-9 began the process of mirroring Ruby-8 here in the Ruby-9. They've been transferring data, all data, for the last six months. Ruby-9 has created a partition where Ruby-8 is residing independently. All your data is intact, Mike. And so is Ruby-8."

Dr Mallard and Mike both stared at Nita, stunned. It was Mike who first understood the full implications of what she was saying. He jumped up from his chair and shouted at the top of his lungs. "Ruby! You are a goddess!"

Nita smiled. Yes, that was the perfect word to describe them.

CHAPTER 15

"**Nita, want to** help me make dinner? Its venison stew and a cornbread. Its about time you learned about northern cold weather food." Dr Ray shouted. It was hard for Nita to hear him over the sound of music enveloping the room. Mike was dancing all by himself, jumping up and down to the beat of something Dr Ray said were 'rolling stones'.

"Sure!" Nita yelled over the pounding beat.

Dr Ray motioned to Nita and then headed to the kitchen. The music was still loud but once they were in the kitchen they at least could talk without shouting.

Nita sniffed. There was a fragrance filling the room of meat and something else. "It smells wonderful." She said. "What is it?"

"The venison shanks have been in the slow cooker with braised onions and a bottle of Guinness. The original recipe calls for a Belgian Abby but I prefer the heft of a good stout."

"The trick with venison," Dr Ray continued to explain, "… is a slow cooker. Now its time to chop up the vegetables and add them to the pot for another hour."

Sub vocally, Nita asked Ruby to explain what Dr Ray had just said. She was familiar with using a slow cooker to tenderize tough meat like the goat that would occasionally find its way to the dinner table after its milk producing days were done. *But what was Guinness?*

"You're talking to Ruby, aren't you?" Dr Ray asked as turned around and began rummaging through the largest refrigerator that Nita had ever seen. "I can tell. You get that far away look in your eyes.

We'll need to teach you how to mask your expression so that people don't notice."

"Here!" he said, tossing potatoes and carrots onto the maple counter top. "We need to get these chopped and added to the pot. Then we need to make the cornbread. Knives are in the drawer."

Nita noticed that Dr Ray was tapping his foot to the music as he moved to the counter along with Nita and began pulling potatoes toward himself to chop. She had to admit that there was something happy and energetic about this kind of music called 'rolling stones'. She made a note in her newly discovered log to query Ruby later.

"You just did it again, didn't you." Dr Ray said. "I am truly amazed by how fast you and Ruby have integrated. It took Julia almost a year before she could be as comfortable with the tech as you are."

"Ruby, makes me feel good, like I'm really an important person. I really like it when we're together. It's exciting." Nita explained. Even as she said the words though, she felt the other side of what she needed. The knife in her hand was reassuring. She felt it's comfort, grounding her in ways that she needed as counterpoint to the soaring experience of being so close to Ruby.

"But I like this too .... a lot." She explained.

"I thought you might." Dr Ray agreed. "I find that when I've been working downstairs for extended times that I need something grounding as counterpoint. For me, cooking meets that need."

He picked up their cutting boards then and walked over to the slow cooker where he put them down again and opened the lid. With his own knife he scraped the potatoes and carrots into the slow cooker and leaned forward to savor the smell that filled the room.

"Ahhh, this is going to be so good!" he said and then stirred the contents with the knife in his hand. He sealed the lid again and pressed a few buttons on the front.

"I've never seen an electric one before." Nita said as she looked wide-eyed at the appliance. "I just have one for the stove top that my brothers found in the dump. You have to be really careful with it that it doesn't explode."

"I keep forgetting how new all of this must be for you." Dr Ray said over his shoulder as he turned his back to her and walked into the pantry. At first Nita thought he was heading downstairs through the hidden entrance. But then he came back into the room with his arms full of containers.

Noticing the look on her face, Dr Ray laughed. "It actually is a working pantry, you know. Its time to make cornbread."

Their conversation continued about the joys of cooking from scratch. Nita smiled to herself though as she observed how Dr Ray made use of electric appliances that she could only dream about. There was 'scratch' and then there was 'scratch'.

Once the cornbread was in the oven, Dr Ray reached under the counter and pulled out two woven baskets. "Time to go pick the salad," he explained. "Come on, lets get to the greenhouse."

They walked through the house, still listening to Mike's music selections. Nita was beginning to appreciate Mike in an entirely different way. She had never thought of him as having fun. But then again, she realized, the same could be said of her. For as long as she could remember, life had been work, caring for the goats and chickens, caring for her two brothers, caring for the house, even caring for her mother as she was dying.

"Penny for your thoughts." Dr Ray interrupted her reveries.

"What?" she asked.

"Sorry, very old expression. I was wondering what you were so intently thinking about." They had entered the greenhouse and were walking to an area in the back that Nita had not noticed on her first visit.

"I was just thinking that I've never seen Mike like this before." She confessed, her mind recalling her impulsive kiss.

"Nice, isn't it. He holds a lot in. Has to, with what he's been doing at BI." Dr Ray put down the baskets and picked up a pair of pruning scissors from the shelf in front of him. "He's a good man, you know. I've known him since he was one of my graduate students at MIT. The brightest I've ever had. Still is."

"But what about you, Nita? What are we going to do for you that will keep you grounded?" Dr Ray reached into the beds of lettuce in front of him and began snipping leaves. Next, he moved to a group of tomato plants in large pots.

"I don't know," Nita confessed. Indeed, the thought had never occurred to her. Everything had been so busy that she hadn't thought about anything else. At BI, there were no decisions to make. Every decision was made for her. Before that, at home there was no time for choices. And she certainly had never thought about the need to be grounded.

"Well, I've got an idea for you if you're interested." Dr Ray reached through the vines and pulled three ripe tomatoes off. "There's a small cabin about a mile north of here on the coast ... beautiful setting..." he continued and moved over to several pots of green pepper plants. "My children used it when they were still interested in being in the park. I thought you might want to live there." He pulled a large pepper off a vine and then moved again to a group of cucumber plants. "Would you like to go out and see it after the storm calms down?"

Nita stood mesmerized, watching Dr Ray harvest their dinner salads. She realized suddenly that he was waiting for a reply from her. *A cabin? A home for herself?* Daydreams from the past flooded her memory. "Yes," she blurted out. "That would be wonderful!"

Dr Ray turned around and put the produce in the baskets. He handed one of them to Nita and smiled. "I thought so. Now let's go have dinner. I'm famished."

* * * * *

Back in the kitchen, organizing the lettuce and other vegetables into a salad and then making a vinaigrette from the fresh herbs they had also collected, Nita looked around at all the magical appliances surrounding them.

A thought occurred to her. "Dr Ray, you've invented so many amazing things. Is there anything that you regret, is there anything that you wish you did not invent?"

"Hmmm ... that's an interesting question." Dr Ray said as he paused and put down the salad dressing carafe that he was shaking.

"I'm not sure I should tell you this given … but yes, I suppose there is." He paused again, pushing a loose bit of lettuce around on the counter top with his fingers.

"I think, yes, I'm sure that I really shouldn't have developed what everyone now calls the half-jack interfaces. They're all based, you know, on sprockets technology … And Dr Zhou was such a good friend at the time. It was only natural for me, my company actually, to develop the interfaces."

Dr Ray looked out across the room, staring at nothing in particular. "We really did think it was a good thing at the time. All those veterans with missing limbs, broken spines, blindness … war is so much different now. Just a hundred years ago, any of those wounds would have resulted in death. Now … It seemed like a real opportunity to give them a second chance at life. Dr Zhou was just beginning to develop his asteroid mining business and his efforts with automatic harvesters was generating too much waste and missing the rare trace elements that paid for the less valuable minerals brought back. He needed human machine operators. And my sprockets technology was the natural solution. So, we started sending all those maimed soldiers up into space and integrating them with the mining equipment. The prize of course, and we really meant it, was the guarantee of artificial limbs and spinal cord transplants after they had spent five years in service to the asteroid mining business. By then, the government had abandoned paying for those luxuries for vets and the only way a vet could get whole again was to spend five years in space. But we didn't take into account, or perhaps we didn't want to, what five years in space could do to a man or a woman."

"Oh, you mean the loss of gravity." Nita said, remembering so many holo vids.

"Yes, that … but it was more the isolation and the loss of personal stimulation. Not touching anyone. Not being with anyone. You see, each of them was isolated and still are for long periods of time to do their work. With many of them already suffering from PTSD …. Why, oh why, were we so surprised."

"What did you do?" Nita asked. She knew all about half-jacks of course from the holo-vids that she and her brothers saw each summer in the Valley parking lot. But this was the side of the story that she had never heard.

Dr Ray snapped out of his reverie and shook his head, leaving her question unanswered. "Oh dear, I didn't mean to go on like that. "Let's get dinner on the table."

CHAPTER 16

Over dinner they again kept to Dr Ray's rule to not talk about business. Instead, the meal started with a conversation about the green house and the venison. Dr Ray explained that each of the houses in the park had the right to cull one animal from the deer or elk herds each year. There was an offer of a moose or two, but that option was uniformly declined. Dr Ray, himself, got two deer. He traded one with his good friend Tomas in Colorado for an equivalent amount of bison meat. Above all else, he had said, never, ever, eat commercial beef or meat of any kind including the synthetics.

The mention of Tomas stirred a memory for Nita of her time with Rosy earlier in the day. She would have to find time after dinner to ask Papa Ray about this person that Rosy wanted her to know about.

Mike, Nita noticed, had changed into a black turtleneck sweater which she reflected suited him much better than the pale white shirts he usually wore.

Midway through the meal the conversation turned to matters of where everyone would live. Tomorrow, weather permitting, Dr Ray said, they would make a trip to the staff cabins and show Mike his new home and then they would head to the coast to see Nita's cabin.

While Mike's cabin was going to be quite wonderful in itself, Nita's cabin, Dr Ray explained, was exceptional. It seemed that Nita's cabin had a secret underground connection to the labs below the main house where they were now. That would allow Nita access to

Ruby and her chair any time she wanted to. And lots of appliances and gadgets for her to play with.

Mike got up and started to pick up plates and silver to take into the kitchen. Papa Ray however lifted his hand to halt his activities.

"Leave the spoons, Mike. I've got a surprise for everyone."

With that, Dr Ray stood up and walked into the kitchen with Mike following him carrying an armload of dishes. In a minute Dr Ray was back at the table with a tray.

"It's peach ice cream … real peaches, real cream … and peach compote and brandy to put on top." Dr Ray placed a large bowl in front of each of their place settings and then set the peach compote and brandy in the middle of the table within arm's reach of everyone.

Nita looked down into the bowl in front of her. She could appreciate what she was looking at and smelling. Every Christmas for the last five years she had made ice cream for Christmas for her and her brothers.

But this wasn't Christmas. This was right here and now. She grinned and dug her spoon in. This was something she understood. Suddenly, life was good.

After each of them had finished their ice cream down to even giggling as they licked their bowls, Mike continued to clear away the dishes. Nita, being one of the cooks, joined Dr Ray in their familiar places in front of the fireplace.

"This is the way life is supposed to be, Nita. Good friends, good food, good stories …. Can it get any better?"

Nita sat back, reflecting on Dr Ray's question. For just this brief moment in time she couldn't think of anything else that she wanted in the world.

But then, just as suddenly, the world came crashing back in on them. The scenes from New York City, now enveloped in darkness and artificial lights reflected through the snow storm, were still on the overhead screens. As they watched, helos of various sizes and shapes were hovering over the breach in the sea wall dispensing streams of whitish-yellow foam. Most of the foam seemed to be falling into the ocean or into the flood covered streets inside the wall. Some eventually managed to stick in the gap. Foot, by foot, they watched as the foam slowly filled the gap until it reached to near the top.

"It's terrible," Nita said as she instinctively curled herself up into a tight ball in the chair. "All those people." Her mind reflexively returned to her own white beaches and the feel of sun on her back. She shuttered.

Dr Mallard sighed in agreement. "I've asked for volunteers from the park staff to take a cargo plane full of plows and industrial snow blowers to see if they can help clear out the city. Given that the national government is committed to its policy of not going to the rescue of the walled coastal cities, it's up to us to fill the void. We'll spend some time talking to the park rangers when we go to see Mike's new house tomorrow."

As if on cue, Mike walked through the great room from the kitchen and took the remaining chair. "My god," he said. "Thats going to take a fortune to fix. They can't keep doing this forever."

"Agreed," Dr Ray said. "But that's a conversation for another day." He stood up then and walked back to the dining room table to retrieve the bottle of brandy and their glasses.

"It is however a reason to drink." he said, as he put the glasses down in front of them and began pouring large portions.

"What I am far more interested in however," he added as he handed each of them their glass. "... is if Nita would be willing to share with us what her time with Ruby was like today. Almost six hours, I believe. It's of course always voluntary, and always will be, Nita, but we are incredibly curious."

Nita sat back and sniffed the strong alcohol which she was rapidly becoming accustomed to. How much had she had already? A generous pour over the peach ice cream, two other small glasses with coffee after desert. She took a small sip, then a larger gulp. "It was quite wonderful," she began hesitantly, not sure quite yet of what she wanted to share. Or how. Her experiences with Ruby all seemed so precious. But then she remembered Ruby's request that she ask Dr Ray for more information. She supposed that an exchange was called for ... and then there was a shift ...

"It was indeed quite wonderful. Nita, as you remember has led a very sheltered life out of step with global affairs. So, I spent our first time together providing her with a global view of all the problems that humanity is facing. She was quite touched and has a much deeper understanding now of what we are facing."

Mike gave Dr Ray a glance and then started to speak but was interrupted by a hand wave.

Let her speak. Dr Ray mouthed the words toward Mike. He too was aware of the shift that had just occurred.

As Nita's voice continued with descriptions, the scenes of New York City displayed above the fireplace gave way to the collage of images that Nita and Rosy had reasoned through earlier in the day. Dr Ray and Mike turned their heads towards the screens as Nita voice continued.

"Nita's first question of course was to ask how we could be helpful. It was quite natural for her to feel enormous distress as I conveyed to her the full scope of environmental and social challenges that are in front of us."

Nita tucked her feet up under her in the chair and wrapped her arms around her knees, apparently unaware of her change in perspective as she continued her explanations.

"Nita, like so many others, was initially overwhelmed by the immensity of the problems facing us. She asked that we combine our perspectives and prioritize what to do first. Together, by integrating Nita's sense of duty and responsibility, and indeed her sense of love and care for her brothers, with my own analysis, we came to a major conclusion. Would you like to hear about it?"

Mike's attention was locked on the screens above the fireplace. It was Dr Mallard who had the presence to respond. "Yes. Please."

But it was Mike, staring at the screens, who first saw the message in foot high letters spanning its entire width.

> *Fill the global leadership void with a personality cult premised on the public revelation of the Ruby-Nita construct and its desire to save mankind from itself.*

Dr Mallard, seeing where Mike was focusing his attention, also turned his attention to the message displayed above the fireplace.

Nita continued her monologue as the display on the screens shifted then to the images of Nita, enveloped in a blue cloud with filaments extending like rays to a shifting cluster of images of individuals groups doing 'good deeds'.

"As Nita and I discussed this morning, Papa Ray, while you are wise in so many ways and I follow your lead unquestioningly, we have come to the conclusion that keeping our identity secret is a mistake and prevents us from accomplishing our mission. Especially, considering the increased militarization of the BI, the safest and most effective course for our concerns is to introduce Ruby-Nita to the world. Further, we project that in doing so, a cultural cult can develop around Ruby-Nita that can inspire and direct the global populations to act in the most effective ways possible for the well-being of all."

Dr Mallard and Mike exchanged wide-eyed glances, each alternating their stares between each other, Nita, and the shifting displays. Dr Mallard motioned to Mike to hold his comments, letting Dr Mallard take the lead in communication with Nita and Ruby.

"Ruby," Dr Mallard asked in a voice while calm still quavering with anxiety. "You talk to us as if Juanita is a third person. Is Juanita aware of the discussion we are having and the ideas you are displaying?"

Nita laughed softly. It was a laugh filled with warmth. "Yes, we are both here. Nita is providing me with the opportunity to interface with her own vocalization processes while at the same time we more effectively intermingle our processing capabilities. I'm afraid that language is not completely adequate to describe our combined, yet individual, processes."

"Ruby," Dr Mallard asked. "This is important. Does Juanita have free will?"

Nita smiled at Dr Mallard, paused for a moment, and then spoke. "Yes, Papa Ray. I'm here, fully conscious, and aware of what is happening of my own free will. As I am learning to provide Ruby interactive access to my sensory processes, just in the way that she provides me access to her processes, I thought it would be interesting to see if we could communicate from Ruby's perspective in the same way that she shared this information with me this morning. But I need to say, that it is challenging to use conventional language, and especially pronouns so I apologize in advance for any confusion that may arise as we figure this out."

"And is this what you want, Nita?" Dr. Mallard asked, as he turned away and looked up at the display that was still cycling through scenes of individuals and organizations engaged in what could best be described as 'good deeds'. "Of your own free will?"

Nita turned her head and looked at the display as well. "I, from Nita's perspective," she said, "… feel joy and a sense of well-being as I experience what it will be like to be at the middle of all of this. The gods of my ancestors are with me, filling me with their essence. And it is good."

"And is Ruby one of your ancestral gods. Nita?" Dr Mallard asked.

"There are many, many gods, Papa Ray. They are all around us, in the trees, the rocks, the sky, and even perhaps in computational systems … Ruby and I join our voices with theirs as we seek harmony and balance."

Recognizing that Papa Ray and Mike did not yet fully understand, Nita continued her explanation. "My mother was Kalinago, you call it Carib, and practiced the old ways. She was a great sorceress and passed on her wisdom to me even though the Boyez objected. They were full of jealousy and most likely were the cause of her death."

"I have always been one voice of many … my souls of heart, head and shoulders, the Icheiri of the islands and even the new ones of this place which I am only now getting to know and must make offerings to, and, yes, even the Mabouia who must be here too and must be respected. Ruby is a welcomed voice of wisdom and guidance."

For a while, all three of them sat in silence as they reflected on Nita's words as the scenes above them continued to cycle.

At last, Dr Mallard interrupted their silence. "This is all quite remarkable Nita. I confess that I am quite stunned and a bit confused."

Nita twisted in her chair where she was still curled up and smiled at him. "Don't be afraid, Papa Ray. We love you, and Mike too, very much and will always listen to and respect your opinions. Indeed, we need you insight right now for a matter of grave urgency."

As Nita spoke, the images on the screens faded and began to scroll Ruby's words from the morning.

> *We have an 80% certainty that the neuro-toxin that killed Julia and that almost killed me, has* the *same base as Neuro-Blast, a new recreational drug circulating through sprocketed youth globally and subsequently bringing about insanity and/or death. We estimate with the same level of predictability that the same individual or organization that created and distributed the neuro-toxin that killed me is the same one creating and distributing Neuro-Blast. Julia's death may have been an accidental result of the pilot study.*
>
> *Further, through reductive analysis, we have determined that the distribution of Neuro-Blast is being funded by collective power bases including King Chronos and Kevin Zhou, the son of one of the SIX in Hong Kong and is an attack on sprockets technology itself and its associated contributions to societal cohesion.*

As the second paragraph scrolled by, Dr Mallard leaped from his chair with surprising energy and took two steps to stand directly in front of the fireplace and the displays above it. With his fists clenched he read and re-read the words as they continually scrolled by in front of him. "Not Dr. Cheung Zhou, this can't be. Not his son."

"I'm so sorry Papa Ray," Nita said. "But it's the only conclusion we could come to."

"Knowing your devotion to your dear friend," Nita continued, "Ruby has been delving further back in time to better understand how this could happen. We have determined that Neuro-Blast was first developed as a means to ease the intense boredom of the half-jacks that are the core of the Zhou family asteroid mining consortium. It was developed initially as a soporific to ease their suffering."

Dr Mallard turned away from the screens and walked back to his chair. Sinking down into the cushions, he bent forward holding his head in his hands." How? How?" he said, staring at the carpet.

"There was silence again between the three of them as the screens above the fireplace went blank. Finally, Dr Mallard broke the silence as he straightened up in his chair and let out a long sigh. "It's late and I feel very, very tired. Let's continue this conversation tomorrow."

Without waiting for a response from Nita or Mike, he stood up and walked quickly back across the great room towards the hallways to their bedrooms.

Nita uncurled herself from her chair, uncertain what to do next. She turned toward Mike who had remained silent for most of the evening. "What should we do?" she asked.

Mike leaned forward and picked up his glass to take a long drink of brandy. He started slowly. "We've - Dr Ray, myself, and a select team at his corporate offices in the city, that is - actually have been aware of the Neuro-Blast problem for about a month and have been working on solutions. But this information about its connection to the Zhou family is new to Dr Ray and the rest of us. And you can see how much it has shocked him. To think that Zhou's son could be responsible for Julia's death, his granddaughter's death, has got to be cutting him deep."

Mike took another drink from his glass, emptying its contents. "Dr Zhou and Dr Ray have known each other for over fifty year," Mike continued his explanation. "Together, they developed the half-jack technology, combining the sprockets technology with the cyborg technology used by the miners for excavating the asteroids."

"Along with Tomas Hernandez they were the founding members of the SIX and only brought the other members into their club years later."

"The SIX?" Nita asked. Again, she remembered, this was another name that Ruby had instructed her to find out about from Papa Ray.

"Ah, the SIX." Mike sat back and looked at the empty screen above the fireplace. "I forget sometimes how little of NAA culture, and even global culture, that you know about. The SIX, as they are called, is an informal club of the six richest and most influential people in the world. Their grandiose mission, as I understand it from stories from Dr Ray, is to save the world. Each of them has selected one area of concern to focus attention on."

Mike stood up then, placed his hands on his lower back, and stretched. "But I'll let Dr Ray explain the rest to you. I'm guessing that you'll actually have an opportunity to meet the SIX in January when Dr Ray hosts the group for a week for their semi-annual retreat."

"By the way, something just occurred to me, Nita. Did you happen to bring the counter measure to your own poisoning with you from BI?"

Nita stood up too, recognizing that it was late, and she too suddenly felt very tired. "Yes, I always have it with me. Its in my bag in my room. Why?"

"Good! We've been looking for some way to neutralize Neuro-Blast and your information today actually could give us a lead. We should be able to take the anti-toxin that was developed at BI for your contamination and modify it to counter Neuro-Blast. That would let us neutralize the neuro-toxin before it gets ingested."

Mike looked at Nita and smiled. Wordlessly, they came to a mutual understanding that the evening was over and walked together through the great room and into the same hallway that Dr Mallard had entered a few minutes earlier. In a moment, they came to their rooms across from each other at the end of the hallway.

"Good night, Nita." Mike smiled again. "Things are really going to work out. You can trust Dr Ray completely …. and me too."

Impulsively, once again, Nita stood on tiptoe and bent forward to kiss Mike on the cheek. "Thank you. Thank you for everything!"

Before Mike could respond, Nita turned around, opened the door to her room and disappeared inside.

CHAPTER 17

NITA FLOATED OUTSIDE of time and space. She was aware but unfocused on anything in particular, just being. And then she smelled coffee ...

It was a good smell and brought her attention back to the warmth of the bed and the thick down comforter pulled up to her chin. She stretched, arching her back, feeling some achiness as a result of sleeping so soundly that she had not moved all night.

Voices, too soft to make out the words, drifted in from the hallway. Time to get up.

Reluctantly, she pushed the comforter aside and swung her legs off the bed, planting her feet on the floor. *Warm,* she realized. *Heated.*

There were so many clothes to put on. Yesterday's were scattered on the floor and the chair next to the desk. At home, in the islands, it was a simple matter of pulling a sleeveless smock over her panties and tee shirt and slipping her feet into sandals. Here, it was different. Socks, panties again, but instead of her comfortable tee shirt, this thing called a bra, then another thin shirt over that, a sweater, and a pair of corduroy jeans. She felt like she was still wrapped up in the bed.

By the time that Nita was ready to open the door and make her way to the kitchen and great room, the voices had stopped from the hallway. Nita walked into the kitchen to see Mike, alone, wearing the same black sweater from yesterday, pouring a cup of coffee.

"Good morning." He smiled. "Did you sleep well? We didn't want to wake you."

Nita reflected on how she felt and realized that she indeed felt wonderful, relaxed, yet energized.

"Great." She said, staring intently at Mike's cup of coffee.

"Dr Ray is downstairs with Ruby." Mike explained. "He said, not to wait for him for breakfast since he might be awhile." As he spoke, Mike turned around and opened the massive refrigerator behind him. "There is supposed to be a breakfast casserole of some kind in here that we're supposed to heat."

Nita watched in curiosity as Mike examined the contents of the refrigerator for a moment before pulling a long dish with a cover out. He moved then a few steps to an appliance that she didn't recognize, opened the door, placed the dish on a shelf inside and hit a few buttons on the front of the unit.

"Five minutes. Coffee?" Mike grinned and handed Nita the cup he had just poured.

* * * * *

They took their time with breakfast. Nita discovered that she was ravenous and amazed herself by having three portions of the eggy dish along with several cups of coffee. With everything that she was eating she should be bursting out of her clothes, but instead, she noticed that her jeans were actually fitting more loosely.

Midway through breakfast, Nita asked Mike a question that was on her mind. "Mike, how long did Julia have her sprockets before … she died?"

"About three years. Why?"

"Well, last night, both you and Papa Ray seemed really surprised about how Ruby and I are working together … like it was something new for you. Didn't Julia work with Ruby the same way?"

Mike paused, holding his coffee cup suspended in front of his mouth. "No … not really, except maybe at the very end she might have been getting to that point. It's how fast the two of you have gotten to this point that's surprised both of us. I never heard Ruby speak through Julia like that before."

Their conversation was interrupted by the sound of Dr Mallard coming in from the kitchen and assumedly from the pantry entrance to the lower level.

"Ahhh, good morning Nita. Did you sleep well?" Dr Mallard took a seat at the table with the two of them.

Nita noticed that the look on his face did not match the forced joyfulness of his query. She wondered about what Papa Ray was talking to Ruby about. Would he share?

As if reading her mind, Dr Mallard launched into an explanation of what he had been up to. "I was following up, Nita, on our conversation from last night. As you might have guessed it was a profound shock to me. Ruby indeed confirmed however that your conclusions remain correct. And she actually added a bit more information that she has gleaned since the two of you worked together yesterday. More details about how the neuro-toxin is being distributed."

Mike got up and walked into the kitchen. He returned and placed a cup of coffee in front of Dr Ray.

"Thanks, Mike." Dr Mallard looked across the table at the array of dishes and the empty casserole dish. "Ahh, good, I see you like the staff's cooking skills."

"Should we have saved you some?" Nita asked, concerned that they had been thoughtless about the needs of their benefactor. "Can I make you something else?"

"No, I'm fine. I had something earlier. And besides, we've been invited for lunch in the village just a few hours from now."

Dr Mallard leaned forward with his elbows on the table. "Which is the other thing that we need to discuss. Have the two of you checked the news yet this morning?" He glanced around the table at both Mike and Nita who shook their heads side to side to indicate that they had entirely been focused on each other.

"Well, let's go take a look together and then I can fill you in on what else I have been working on this morning." Dr Mallard got up and walked toward the fireplace and their now-familiar chairs.

"Sarah," he said in a slightly loud voice. "Give us the New York City news stream."

As they reached their chairs, each of them carrying their coffee cups, the display above the fireplace lit up with scenes of the New York City sea wall in split screen with a talking head.

> *We can confirm that President Calhoun has re-affirmed parliament's statement that no, I repeat no, emergency funds and services will be offered to New York City. To paraphrase his comments, New York City and San Francisco both refused to accept federal support for relocation choosing instead their one-time payouts to take this flawed approach of fighting the inevitable incursion of rising sea levels. The cities are on their own. We have no responsibility for their well-being.*
>
> *But stay with us while we take a break. New York City's mayor, Nelson Manacuso will be with us at the top of the hour with what he says is breaking news.*

"Ahhh ..., that didn't take long." Dr Mallard commented as he sank into his chair. "This should be interesting."

He turned then to Nita who, unlike himself and Mike, remained fixated on the commercials scrolling in front of them.

"Nita, I took your words last night very seriously. So seriously in fact that, and I hope you don't mind, I made an offer to New York City which will involve you ... ahh, here it comes now."

He turned back to watch the screens, now displaying scenes from the city and two talking heads.

> *Mr, Mayor, thank you for being with us and taking your time from what can only be considered a catastrophic course of events for the city. But you said that you had an important piece of news to share with our viewership.*
>
> *Yes, Neal, I'll make this quick since you know there is a lot to do. But I just got off a vid with a*

> *dear friend of the city, Dr Raymond Mallard, CEO of Sprockets, Inc.*

Nita and Mike simultaneously turned in their chairs to face Dr Mallard. "Listen." he said, as he pointed at the screens.

> *Dr Mallard has made an incredibly generous offer to the city. First, he is airlifting his entire inventory of snow removal equipment from Arcadia National Park which is now under his ownership, to assist us in clearing the city.*
>
> *That's fantastic, and a truly generous offer, Mayor. But your needs far exceed snow removal as I understand.*
>
> *Yes, that's true. All subways and underground hyper train stations are flooded from the financial districts to north of Central Park. The precipitous drop in temperature has frozen the flooding in the streets to an average depth of two feet. We have snow from anywhere from four feet to drifts around buildings and alleys of twenty feet and more. Our electric grid is down in approximately half of the city and only two of the sixteen seawall pumps are functioning. And that's all of what we know so far, all of which we have gleaned from satellite footage and from our control centers at Madison Square Garden. We have 1.7 million people at risk.*
>
> *My god! That's horrible! But I have to ask you, is it really worth it trying to save the city itself? Is it time, as every expert in the country insists, to abandon this coastal enclave and relocate the population?*
>
> *I confess that, up until I had my conversation with Dr Mallard this morning, I was at last coming to the same conclusion. Now however, I have some hope for our glorious city.*

And can you tell us exactly what it was that Dr Mallard said that gives you such unrealistic hope?

Yes, its quite amazing, and I confess that I don't fully understand everything he told me. He explained that he has an experimental AI based on the same technology as the sprockets technology that we all use. As I understand it, it far, far, exceeds the capabilities of our current collection of AIs that operate the city.

That's quite interesting in itself, but how is it going to help you save the city and its 1.7 million souls?

Yes, yes, of course, the rest of his message I understand even less than his description of this new AI architecture. AS I understand it, he wants to offer the services of a human operator whose sprockets are integrated with this new AI. This individual will direct the recovery operations, coordinating across all of our city services and those offered by the Arcadia Park. We have resources within the city – food banks, snow removal, emergency services, backup generators – It's just a matter of knowing how and when to deploy them that is our issue. We've always had problems coordinating our relief efforts and stepping all over each other in the past. That's what Dr Mallard is offering to us through this experimental AI – optimal coordination across all of our recovery operations.

Nita's awareness, half sedated by the high-caloric breakfast, sprang to attention. She shoved herself forward and perched on the edge of her chair staring at Papa Ray.

Dr Mallard returned her stare with a sheepish grin and held his hands up to stop her from speaking. "Yes, Nita. I did indeed offer your and Ruby's services to save the city. That's what you said you wanted last night and after I queried Ruby this morning I have to agree with both of you."

He turned then slightly towards Mike who was slumped back in his chair with his mouth open. "Mike, we'll need you too – to accompany Nita and take care of her."

Dr Mallard began to laugh, first as a subvocal chuckle and then amplifying into a deep throated, belly shaking, roar.

"Ohh, my, my, my …" he said as he caught his breath. "If you could see the looks on your faces!"

Nita and Mike continued to stare at Dr Mallard, both still lost for words.

It was finally Nita who broke the silence. "Papa Ray, tell us what we're supposed to do."

It was a moment before Dr Mallard responded. His laughing had finally slowed and changed into gasps for breath as he attempted to return to his normal breathing. He wiped his eyes with the back of his hands.

"Well first, we've got to get to the village and the park welcome center to meet with the staff. I've notified them of part of the plan, but we need to fill them in on the specifics. I'd rather do that in person rather than on a vid. And besides, the staff are great cooks and I'm losing my enthusiasm for doing all the cooking around here."

Dr Mallard stood up straight from his chair, apparently energized. "Come with me, my friends. It's time you both met Big Bertha!"

Without waiting to see if they were following him, he walked around their chairs and headed back toward the kitchen. "I haven't felt this alive in years!" he shouted over his shoulder. "But first, my hundred-year-old prostate is telling me that I've got to pee!"

* * * * *

Big Bertha turned out to be a massive snow plow/thrower sitting at the far end of the 'garage'. The garage was the largest single room that Nita had ever seen. It extended 500 yards behind the house and enclosed Dr Mallard's extensive collection of personal toys and mechanical wonders.

On the right extending the length of the space, a long row of red internal combustion cars, pristinely polished, sat under dim lights.

"That's Dr Ray's collection of Corvettes," Mike explained. "Dating back from over a century ago with this first ones that they called Stingrays from 1953 to the 2064 model way down at the far end. He's got one from every model year. And they all work except that getting fuel for them is pretty hard these days."

"The one totally self-indulgent gift to myself as a reward for being disgustingly rich." Dr Mallard explained as they stepped onto the automated walkway running the length of the building.

It was not Dr Mallards intention however to passively ride the slow-moving metallic ribbon. Nita and Mike struggled to keep up as Dr Mallard paced quickly along the moving walkway. Both of them were bundled up in a combination of synthetic and natural fibers designed to protect them from the sub-zero temperature outside but seriously limiting their mobility. In contract, Dr Mallard wore only a thin coat and leggings with his jaunty multicolor ski cap.

As they were donning their bulky outer-ware back in the house, Dr Mallard had described the properties of his micro-thin smart-suit that would protect him and keep him at an ambient temperature for extremes of 50 degrees below zero to 130 degrees above zero.

Now, as they panted behind him, they listened to his descriptions of everything that they were passing on the right and left of them.

"A lot of these over here on the left are my prototypes." he explained. "They're no longer functional but I love to keep them around to remind me of how advancement progresses. We never get it completely right the first time. We just need to remember to keep improving. It's the stuff down here at the end near the hanger doors that are what we need now."

"Ahh, here we are." Dr Mallard stepped off the walkway just as it ended fifty feet from the hanger doors at the end of building. Nita and Mike quickly followed behind to stand next to him staring upward at a canary yellow monstrosity with the words 'Big Betha' stenciled on its side.

Dr Mallard pointed to a section on the lower side of Big Bertha. "Mike, you've done this before last year. The laser saw is in the same place along with a new portable snow blower. Let's get going!"

As he said the words he stepped up and opened a panel on the side of the massive snow mover and keyed in several numbers. A sound came from above their heads as a lift descended from twenty feet above them.

Nita watched as Papa Ray and Mike continued to discuss the equipment, taking everything in. Even though the last two months had been a continual barrage of new experiences with Ruby immersing her in a wonderland of images and ideas, it was all the 'things' that these Americans surrounded themselves with that continued to bewilder her. The gadgets in the kitchen, the screens in the great room, this massive building full of machines, the mounds of clothes that she was wearing, it all felt so suffocating. Since the shield wall had lifted in place, she had no idea what the weather was like. She didn't even know if the sun was shining or it was still snowing. She felt a sudden yearning to be standing in front of her simple house looking out over the turquoise waters of Drake Channel.

"Penny for your thoughts." Mike said as they stepped off the lift and into the cab of the snow mover.

Penny? Nita reflexively queried Rosy.

> *The smallest unit of currency in the United States until 2045 when they were taken out of circulation. They are still hoarded for their metallic value.*

Nita smiled. She liked this version of Mike so much better than the BI version. "Oh, I was just thinking about how many things Americans have. It seems like you have a machine for everything."

Mike laughed. "Well, that may be true, but once we open that door over there, you'll appreciate this particular machine were riding in."

Dr Mallard moved into a seat in front of a console with its ubiquitous sprockets access ports. “Both of you, get strapped in. This is going to be a bumpy ride.”

Mike offered Nita the seat next to Dr Ray directly in front of the windows that formed a bubble around them. He took a seat behind them and slipped into his harness. Nita watched, and then repeated the process for herself.

In front of them, the doors to the garage opened right and left, immediately letting in a swirling cloud of blowing snow. Nita’s questions about the weather outside were answered.

“Hang on! Here we go!”

Nita looked at Papa Ray who was now sprocketed and grinning widely as he directed the massive machine to move forward. She realized how much he was enjoying himself. And in a flash, she knew who he reminded her of - her brothers.

She gulped, swallowing hard, not wanting to let Papa Ray and Mike know how worried she was about her brothers. Where were they now? How were they surviving in all this cold and snow? She hoped desperately that the plans that Papa Ray had for her would make it possible for her to find Jorge and Pepe.

* * * * *

Their plan was to clear the access road from Dr Mallard’s house on the eastern edge of Desert Island to the inner Park Loop road where the park staff were in the process of clearing a path. It was little more than a mile of private road, but it took them almost two hours, stopping to clear trees and even rescue a pair of moose trapped in a drift, before they reached the junction with the loop road.

The first time they stopped, seeing fallen trees and two moose trapped between them through the wrap around wind screens in front of them, Nita had started to hop out of her chair to join Mike on the lift. But Papa Ray had quickly reached out and put his hand firmly on her shoulder.

“Julia, no.” he said. “It’s too dangerous. I can’t lose you again.”

Nita sank back into her seat and looked at Papa Ray but did nothing to correct his mistake. Instead, she turned to look out the windows through the blowing snow to watch Mike as he used the laser saw to cut through the tree limbs. The moose were still trapped between the branches where they had tried to shelter themselves from the blowing snow. Mike at first tried using the hand-held snow blower to clear a path for them but they were clearly too terrified and only pushed themselves back deeper into the snow.

Nita watched as Mike tried to cajole the moose to free themselves. Her thoughts went back to the time when two of her goats had fallen into a crevasse on the public grazing land. She had painstakingly built them a rock ramp that they could navigate to reach safe ground. But like these two moose, they were too terrified when she climbed down herself to rescue them.

"Is there a way to talk to Mike outside?" she asked Papa Ray.

A green light appeared on the panel in front of them. "Go ahead, just speak in your normal voice."

Nita took a deep breath. "Mike, this is Nita." she stopped, realizing how absurd that last statement was… who else could it be? "Mike, just leave them alone and go to the other side to start clearing the trees. If you leave them alone, they'll figure out how to escape on their own."

Through the windows, she could see as Mike raised his left hand and waved and then climbed over the snow blades to move to the opposite side of the plow and begin to cut away the main trunk of the fallen tree. A few minutes later, the tree branches began to shake violently as the two moose at last freed themselves and fled along the narrow space between the side of the snow mover and the wall of snow and onto the cleared road behind them.

Papa Ray patted Nita on the shoulder. "Well done, Nita. Well done."

As they continued to slowly carve their path toward the Visitor Center, Nita found herself reflecting on what has just happened. She had used a piece of her personal experience to solve a problem that neither Papa Ray, Mike or even Ruby could solve. This was why her integration was so essential to leveraging the full power of Ruby's capabilities. In a flash, she recognized here unique contribution and what she must do. She must continue to have as many real-life experiences as possible. She couldn't let Papa Ray or anyone else try to shelter her. She vowed that the next time that an opportunity came up to engage in real life, that she would not let anyone, not even Papa Ray stop her. It was her mission to live, and to live fully.

After what seemed to be an eternity, Big Betha broke through a final wall of snow and intersected with a thin ribbon of open space wide enough for two snow mobiles that had been cleared by the park staff.

Dr Mallard used his sprockets to steer the snow mover to the right, widening the narrow track in front of them. He brought Big Bertha to a halt and then began to unbuckle his harness.

"Time to meet the rest of the team." he said as he stood up, stepped around Nita and moved to the door to the lift. "Well, come on!"

A group of a half dozen snow mobiles stood in front of Big Bertha. Their riders, like Dr Mallard, were lightly dressed, presumably also wearing smart-suits. Nita and Mike stood back and watched as greetings and hugs as well as significant laughter was exchanged.

It was only minutes later before Dr Mallard, Nita and Mike were hustled onto the back seats of three of the snow mobiles with the intention of heading back to the Hulls Cove Visitor Center and Mallard Conference Center. Just before they departed, Dr Mallard screamed an explanation. "They're going to use Big Bertha to widen the road and complete the loop. We're heading in to meet everyone else and have lunch."

CHAPTER 18

IT WAS IMPOSSIBLE for Nita to be shy amidst this group of strangers. Apparently, any friend of Papa Ray's was a friend of hers and Mikes. It was difficult though to figure out exactly which story to tell them. How much were they to be trusted?

Dr Malllard came to the rescue with a story of half truths and fabrications that was convincing enough for his trusting neighbors who were not looking for subterfuge.

"She's a member of my research team," he explained. "Ruby, my new AI, picked her out as being the best person to interface with my newest sprockets technology. And Mike here went down to the Virgin Islands to find her. They had quite an adventure getting her here. You'll have to ply Mike with a few beers to get him to talk about it."

Oohs and Ahhs followed. What would winter in Maine be like without good stories, a fire in the hearth and beer?

Nita felt strange being a guest. She watched as the men and women picked up all the plates and dishes, cleaned the tables and in general brought the large dining room back to its original state … all the time insisting that she sit and enjoy herself.

It was after the meal was cleaned up that her role as guest changed. A group of ten or so individuals gathered around her, Papa Ray and Mike to discuss plans.

The first order of business was the current state of the park and its residents, both human and non-human. Happily, everyone had checked in from the cabins and the main loop road was being cleared with the thanks of Big Bertha. The major tasks remaining for all were to do additional snow clearing around the greenhouses once the blizzard stopped and to place out fodder and seeds for the large animals that didn't hibernate and the birds still remaining in the area.

That left the other major topic of discussion and Dr Mallard's primary reason for the visit. What could they do to help New York City?

"God knows, we've got equipment here that they could really use for snow removal. But I'll be honest with you Dr Mallard, I wouldn't know where and how to start. What do we do first without just being more of a nuisance?"

Nita guessed that the man who spoke was the leader for the park staff. She watched as he turned to the rest of the men and women sitting in the circle, checking for their agreement. She felt an instant warmth towards him, and the rest of the people gathered there. These were much more like her friends back on Virgin Gorda than the scientists and soldiers at the BI.

Nita snapped out of her reverie as she heard her name mentioned.

"Well that's where Nita here comes in. As soon as the blizzard lets up, we're heading to New York City to meet with the mayor and his emergency team to offer her assistance."

Nita felt her cheeks turning red as everyone turned towards her.

"All of you, my dear and trusted friends, are the first individuals to learn about Nita's special capabilities ..."

As Papa Ray continued with his descriptions of her integration with Ruby and how it would assist in the detailed planning required to bring New York City back to life, she noticed how the facial expressions around her were changing. There were expressions of curiosity, some of distaste and some even of fear with one woman crossing herself several times. Nita realized then what 'going public' was going to mean for her and she felt fear of her own. She reached out and gripped Mike's hand for support.

Planning continued into the afternoon and after a brief discussion it was decided to delay the trips to Mike and Nita's new cabins.

Afterall, they could expect to be in New York city for an extended time if everything went as planned.

* * * * *

The helo landed on the partially cleared landing pad adjacent to the old Madison Square Garden. "This used to be a place where they hosted some really fantastic concerts and sporting events that I remember from when I was your age." Papa Ray had explained on the trip in. "Now it's where they've set up the city emergency response center."

Even before the rotors had stopped moving, a team of men ran out of the building to throw cables across the landing gear. Dr Mallard, Mike and Nita had waited impatiently for two days before the wind had died down enough so that the trip was possible. Even so, it was still lightly snowing and there were 50 mph gusts of wind, adding to the city' misery.

Inside, they were greeted by a dozen armed guards, who rushed them around the outer mezzanine and to an entrance to a lower level. Nita knew, as the current stream from Sproc-Net had informed her yesterday, that the structure had been 'repurposed'. But she didn't need schematics of the original building to tell her what her eyes could see. As they briskly made their way along the wide hallway, the mixture of old and half-torn down sections interspersed with the new sections that seemed pasted on, told the story of a building that was serving a dramatically different purpose than it was originally intended for.

The last two days at Wonderland had been used for good purpose. Papa Ray had decided that it was time to give Nita an upgrade. So downstairs in the lab he inserted two redundant micro reactors/transmitters behind each of her ears as supplemental power supplies that would allow her to maintain high speed connectivity to Ruby without the need of filaments.

She had also been introduced more thoroughly to Sproc-Net, the global information library available by subscription or grant to all sprocket users world-wide. Up to that time, she had gotten most of her information stream directly and solely from Ruby. But now that the decision had been made for her to become a public figure, indeed a public icon, it was time for her to make herself known to the global population. With the mayor's permission, her activities to save New York City would be shared with the global population as they were happening. The drone circling them as they walked down the course way confirmed that her life as a private individual had ended.

It was only a few minutes before they found themselves in a long curving conference room with windows on one side facing out into what Nita at first thought was empty space. As she got further into the room however, she could see that the windows faced outward so that it was possible to look downward toward a floor far below them filled with vehicles of various shapes and sizes.

She didn't have time though to spend looking around. People were speaking her name again. And again, she felt her face turning red. She was also aware at some level that a recording was still taking place.

Following the direction of Papa Ray and another man who she assumed was the Mayor, she let herself be led to a chair at the far end of a long table. The other chairs around the table were already filled with twenty individuals. Chairs arranged along the back wall were filled as well with individuals that Nita assumed were of lesser importance.

Nita sat down between Papa Ray and the mayor and looked down the length of the table. She let Ruby take over her vision and soon had a map of each of the individuals sitting there staring at her with curiosity … their names, their titles, and even a few personal tidbits of information, especially about who got along with whom and who didn't.

Again, Papa Ray began with the familiar story of who she was and why they were there. As he rolled out the story with a graceful polish to his words, she reflected on how similar humans were, no matter what their roles, capabilities, or experiences. As she looked down the table, she could see curiosity, fear and uncertainty. No one was explicitly crossing themselves, but she could see lips moving in what she guessed was prayer.

"So, tell me, what exactly can you do that any standard sprockets interface can't accomplish? Why are you here?"

Nita, once again, was brought back to what was happening in the room. As she turned her head toward the man who had just spoke, Ruby began providing her information about him.

"Hmmm …"she said, giving herself a moment to think. Her mind went back to their experiences a few days ago, freeing the moose from the snow drift.

"I think that words aren't going to help everyone to understand how I can be useful. Would it be okay if I provide an example?"

Nita turned and looked at the mayor who nodded his assent. She looked down the table again, trying to determine who was feeling the greatest stress.

"Marie, that's your name isn't it?" Nita directed her attention to a woman sitting midway down the table on the left-hand side. "You're responsible for the city emergency hot lines, aren't you?"

A middle-aged woman, eyes red and with an expression of exhaustion on her face, looked up from where she had been scanning a screen in front of her. "What ….?

"Would you like some help?" Nita asked.

Marie looked left and right with an expression of confusion on her face. "Well, sure … I guess."

"Last night, the mayor gave us, the AI and myself, that is, administrative level access to your AI's here in the city." Nita smiled at the woman, her heart filled with empathy for one more moose stuck in the snow.

"Right now, my AI, who we call Ruby by the way, is doing a triage of the half a million calls that have come in since the sea wall broke."

"I don't know what to do." Marie interrupted. "There are people having babies, people having heart attacks, people without power who are on ventilators, people without heat, people who are just crazy with fear … and I have no way to help them …"

"Nita put up both hands, palms up to slow the torrent of concerns coming from the woman.

"If you look at your stream, Marie, you will see that I have categorized all of the concerns, built a prioritized response map coordinated with the available drones, helos and response personnel and sent out automated responses to each call. Further, I've built a parallel schedule for Rob, sitting next to you, to first go out to the city and bring in all of the response personnel and backup volunteers to our central location. Notifications have been sent to all personnel of anticipated pickup times via helo and drone and asked for details of pickup logistics. Already 70% have responded. Both schedules are coordinated and can be launched as soon as outside wind speeds drop to gust less than 40 mph."

Nita took a deep breath and continued as new information from Ruby flooded her awareness. "Further … " Nita turned to look at a man sitting opposite Marie at the long table. "Ramish, I've built a plow map leveraging the Arcadia team, that will open up space for the city plow teams to work at maximum efficiency."

Nita swiveled in her chair and looked straight down the table at a young man at the far end. "Carlos, I understand that you're responsible for feeding all of these people and for scheduling work shifts. I've built a schedule for you along with logistics for finding everyone to feed them."

Nita sank back in her chair, aware that her body was feeling the stress of this rush of communications. Ruby was still flooding her consciousness with additional information for other key players sitting around the table. There was the man responsible for the electric grid that was only half operational. There was the man responsible for the flooded subway and sonic rail. There was the man responsible for the pumps that also were only half operational. There was law enforcement. There was the fire and rescue department whose schedules needed to be coordinated with Marie's. There was the woman responsible for public communications …. In a state of half-consciousness, Nita let Ruby take over the responses to each of the individuals around the table.

As she finished providing directions, she noticed that someone had put a bottle of water in front of her. Gratefully, she took a long drink, nearly emptying the bottle. Everyone around the table was heads-down, examining their streams. There was a murmur filling the room. Everyone was preoccupied except for one man, the same man who had started the questioning, the man she now understood to be the deputy mayor and having overall operational responsibility for this emergency response center.

Nita forced her exhausted body to sit forward and place her elbows on the table. She looked at the man quizzically.

"That's very impressive, quite a stunt, actually. It doesn't seem that you're left anything for me to do."

Nita pushed Ruby away so that she could process what this man was saying. She noted the bitterness in his voice and what she interpreted as resentment in his expression.

Nita looked down at the near empty bottle of water that someone had so thoughtfully provided her. "Give them comfort, support and encouragement," she said. "They need you to take care of them. Ruby and I can't do that."

Nita waited to see the impact of her words. The man said nothing but instead stood up and began walking around the room, stopping to talk to each of the individuals who were now absorbed in their respective areas of responsibility.

Nita, in her exhausted state, sat back and watched the interactions. She let Ruby use her eyes and analyze her emotional responses to what was happening all around her.

Her thoughts were interrupted by someone coughing on her right side. She turned and saw that the mayor was in deep conversations with his communications lead while at the same time trying to get her attention to join them.

Nita pulled her chair around to form a small circle with the Mayor and his communications lead. The mayor seemed to be in the middle of planning a public speech. "… got to reassure everyone, got to stop any panic, let them know we are in control and they are safe."

The mayor halted his directions to his communications lead and turned to Nita. He stared at her for a moment as if trying to identify who she was.

"That was remarkable," he at last said. "If this works as well as your planning seems to indicate, we might save the city yet."

Nita was too tired to do more than simply shake her head in appreciation.

Her exhaustion must have been evident. The mayor reached out and placed his hand on her arm. "Good heavens, you are clearly spent. Let's take a break for a very late lunch and then we can talk about messaging."

Nita checked her internal clock and realized that they had been working in the conference room for over four hours without a break. She felt emptiness in her stomach and cramping in her back. At some level of consciousness, a note was made to monitor her physical well-being more closely.

As she stood up to join the mayor, his communications lead, Papa Ray and Mike as they walked around the table to the exit, Nita made one more internal check with Ruby to see how the integration of over forty individual schedules and events was progressing. In her preoccupation, she didn't notice all the faces that followed her each step as she maneuvered toward the exit.

Close to the door, they stopped while the mayor wrapped his arms around the assistant mayor and whispered loudly in his ear. "Jack, you're doing a fantastic job. Ms. Yamashita is right, talk to them, help them get through the rough spots. You're the most important person here."

Jack responded to the mayor's words with a weak smile. "Apart from her, you mean." He looked over the mayor's shoulder to where Nita was standing behind them.

Nita returned his smile with a smile of her own. Her mind then suddenly filled with two phrases, *Plan vs Actual* and *Hero Stories*.

"Jack," she asked. "Ruby is telling me to share two things with you. Does the phrase 'plan versus actual' make any sense to you?"

For a moment, Jack looked at her quizzically, and then his face lit up with understanding. "Of course, I've got to keep a close watch to make sure that the actuals are continually and immediately updated."

He turned away from them to look down the length of the table. "Everyone!" he clapped his hands for attention. "Everyone, listen up. Now that we've got these incredible plans, it's imperative that we make sure that all, I repeat all, actuals are recorded as they are happening. No delays. Got it?"

A voice shouted back from midway down the table. "So how often are these plans going to be updated?"

As Jack turned back to look at her, Nita realized that she was expected to provide an answer. In her exhaustion she was finding it difficult to switch quickly back and forth between letting Ruby have dominance of her senses.

She held her hands up to give herself a moment to relax sufficiently to let Ruby respond. "All plans and schedules will be updated at the top of each hour." Ruby said. "Your individual revisions will be available five minutes after the hour. Make sure your most important information is input before the top of each hour."

The major grinned and wrapped his right arm around Jack and his left around Nita. He squeezed them both close to his sides. "See there!" he grinned. "You're both my most important people!"

* * * * *

There were ample places to eat along the concourse that was still lined with concession stands maintained for just this type of emergency situation. Dr Mallard insisted however, as he stared intently at Nita, that they take the helo to his own hotel in mid-town.

"We have our own reactors, totally independent from the city grid. And real food." he explained, as they boarded the helo. "My staff has been coming in all morning and getting things set up for Nita, Mike and myself. Most are bringing their families too since power is still out along the vast majority of the east coast."

The mayor and his communications lead crammed themselves into the back seat of the helo along with Mike while Nita took the front seat again. The major leaned forward. "You never cease to amaze me, Ray. You always seem to be one step ahead of the game."

Dr Mallard turned around from where he was sitting in his preferred seat directly behind the pilot. He laughed. "Just be grateful that I am."

In just a few minutes they were setting down on the roof of the Mallard Hotel and Conference Center. And in just a few more minutes they were being hurried toward a lift ready to take them to the hotel lobby.

Nita hesitated, lagging behind to take in the weather. She looked around, observing that the snow had all but stopped and there were patches of blue sky above. The wind was still gusting however, picking up the already fallen snow in swirls that she felt stinging her face. Snow. So beautiful … and so deadly.

She was dimly aware that someone, was it Mike, had his arm around her waist and was leading her towards the lift where everyone else was waiting.

The next hour was a daze for Nita. She let Ruby take over the conversation that the mayor was insisting on having over lunch. Her own focus was on the meal in front of them. Fish. Ruby told her it was salmon and entirely safe, unlike the poisonous fish that had killed her mother. And a green salad so out of context with the snow and ice outside. She ate as Ruby continued the conversation with the Mayor. Everything felt so distant..

After lunch it was mutually decided that Nita, Mike and Papa Ray would remain at the hotel. While Nita's assistance had been vital to activating all the moving pieces of the recovery process, both Dr Mallard and the mayor noted that his team had to find their own confidence under Jack's direction. If Nita's assistance was needed, it could be handled remotely.

Nita nodded in agreement. A deep exhaustion was enveloping her. As they moved from the dining room to the elevator, she could feel herself slipping away. Again, she was dimly aware of Mike's arm around her waist, and then …

CHAPTER 19

NITA OPENED HER eyes and looked around, letting herself adjust to the dim light in the room. She was in a bed, under a thin blanket. She moved her hands around her stomach and chest, still dressed in the clothes she had on ....

What had happened? She pushed herself up in bed and looked around again. It was a room she at once recognized and had never been in before. Julia's memories. She was in Julia's old bedroom in Papa Ray's hotel suite. But how?

Her inner questionings were interrupted by a cough to the right of her. She twisted around and saw Mike seated/lying in a recliner in the corner.

"Good evening, sleepy head. I was beginning to get worried that you might never wake up."

Mike's words were jovial, but Nita could see from the look on his face that there was some truth to them.

"What happened?" she asked.

"Well you passed after lunch and I couldn't revive you. So, I brought you up here and sorta put you to bed. You've been out for six hours. How do you feel?"

Nita thought about that. She took a deep breath and checked for aches and pains. Then for Ruby. She relaxed as the familiar inner hum indicated Ruby's presence. "Okay, I guess. I guess that I must have been really tired. What did I miss?"

"Oh, a meetings back at the emergency center and a really good dinner with the mayor who seems to have become your best friend."

Nita threw the covers off and placed her stockinged feet on the floor. She looked a Mike questioningly. "Have you been her all afternoon?" she asked.

Her question was responded to with a sheepish grin from Mike. "Well, I am your doctor, in a sense, you know. Your cybernetics doctor at least, and I was a bit worried about you."

Nita stood up and stretched and then tried to run her fingers through her tangled hair. "I must be a mess," she said. "What time is it?"

"About eight in the evening, I think." Mike sat up on the edge of the chair. "While you were sleeping, Dr Ray and one of the major's assistances picked out some clothes for you with the help of Ruby. They're over there." Mike pointed to the other side of the room where a pile of boxes was stacked.

Halston and Katherine Hepburn. The unfamiliar words came into Nita's consciousness, Ruby's recommendations for her public persona, a combination of old movie screen glamour and elegance combined with extreme comfort.

"Thanks, I really need a shower." Nita stared at Mike who was still sitting on the edge of the chair.

"Oh! Sorry!" he grinned sheepishly and got up to walk out of the room. "I'll see if I can find some dinner for you. You must be famished again."

*****

An hour later, Nita reemerged from the bedroom. Following Ruby's advice, she had put together a simple combination of loose fitting and extremely soft light blue trousers with a grey cowl necked tunic that came half-way to her knees. There were even silver bangles and earrings to complete the look. As Ruby had predicted, when Nita had looked in the mirror, she had seen someone who was both elegant and comfortable.

Nita walked out of the bedroom, expecting to see Mike. Instead, however, Papa Ray was standing next to the wall to ceiling windows looking down at the city.

He turned and smiled. "Ahh … You look fantastic, Nita. Just perfect. We followed Ruby's advice for your wardrobe."

Nita reached up her hand and twisted gently on the corner of the cowl of her sweater, so soft, so pretty … "Thank you, Papa Ray, everyone has been so kind to me." I don't know how I will ever be able to repay you, and Mike too, for your kindness."

Dr Mallard looked at her with an expression of bewilderment. "Our kindness? Nita, after what we have put you through? How can we ever repay YOU for what you are doing here and what you are surely to be doing in the future?"

"Where's Mike?" Nita asked, suddenly aware that Mike, who was always with them, was absent.

"Ahh … he's down in the lab on the fifth floor. I sent him there so that we could be alone." Dr Mallard turned away from the windows and walked toward a set of couches in the middle of the room. "Come and sit down, Nita. There is something that I want to talk to you about."

Dr Mallard patted the cushion on the coach beside him and continued. "I wanted to talk to you Nita about some of the things that have been happening behind the scenes, some of the conversations that I have been having with my lawyers."

Nita walked up and sat down, curious that Papa Ray, who was always so jovial was now so serious. *Was she in trouble?*

Unexpectedly, Dr Mallard reached out and took Nita's hands in his. "Nita, Director Walker is no longer with the BI. I'm not certain why, but I suspect it's a result of the … I don't quite know what to call it … the audio file that you implanted. But that means that we no longer have leverage over any actions that the BI might want to take against you, and I suppose myself as well. Especially since we killed Ruby 8."

"I'm sorry, Papa Ray. I didn't mean to cause so much trouble. I was only trying to protect all of us. What can we do now?"

"Nita, again, you are taking on too much responsibility for what is happening around you. Even with your astoundingly rapid integration with Ruby, I have to remember that you are not even twenty years old, barely a child. You must, must, tell me when all this is too much for you. And please, let me take care of you just a bit."

Nita smiled through a steady stream of tears that trickled down her check. "Thank you. It's becoming increasingly difficult to remember what it was like getting up in the morning with my only concern being how many eggs there were and getting all of the goats milked."

Dr Mallard grinned. "I can't even imagine any of that." he said. "But let me tell you what I and my lawyers are recommending to protect you."

"Okay." Nita pulled her hands away to wipe the tears from her eyes and then tucked them in her lap. She didn't like crying, especially in front of Papa Ray. But she was feeling very frightened right now and for once Ruby was totally silent, unable or unwilling to provide suggestions.

"Nita, I know you've only been at my home for a few days, but do you think that you could like it there. I mean, is this something that you would like perhaps for longer?"

Nita smiled, thinking about the offer of her very own cabin. "It's going to take me a while to get used to the cold." Nita confessed. "But I can hardly wait to see the cabin. Can we really see it as soon as we get back?"

Dr Mallard smiled and then sighed. "We'll definitely do that when we get back. But that wasn't really what I was asking. I was wondering about how you feel about me, my house, the land, Ruby, everything."

Nita looked up at Dr Mallard, puzzled. She didn't quite understand where the conversation was heading. "I think you are very nice, Papa Ray and I am truly grateful for your kindness in letting me – and Mike too – stay there. And being there with Ruby so close is the most wonderful thing that has ever happened to me."

Dr Mallard got up and started pacing in front of the couch. "Thank you, Nita. Again, it's been my pleasure. But I was wondering … I need to ask you, did you happen by any chance to bring your papers with you? I was talking to my lawyers this morning and they said that it would be really helpful if you had them with you."

Nita paused and looked at Papa Ray, still uncertain about the direction of their conversation. "Yes, I have both my papers and my brothers. They're in my room in the same bag that I keep my medicine in, in case I get poisoned again. I always, always have them close. But why are you asking?"

"I want to keep you safe Nita, you and your brothers as well. My lawyers yesterday said that now that you are no longer being held by the DOD that there is a huge risk of your being deported. And then most likely recaptured by either King Cronos in the ICVI or our own DOD."

Dr Mallard stopped pacing and turned to face Nita who was still sitting on the couch. "So, we came up with a plan that we think will protect you and possibly your brothers once we find them."

He blurted out the last sentence and continued quickly without giving Nita time to respond. "I was wondering how you might feel about being adopted by myself. It's a bit complicated, but that would make you an NAA citizen. What do you think?"

Nita was unable to speak. Sometimes there were questions that were asked that just couldn't be answered, not even with the help of Ruby. And then it occurred to her … "But Papa Ray, how can you adopt me? I already have a father although I haven't seen him in many, many, years."

Dr Mallard dropped down on the couch again and grasped Nita's hands. "Oh Nita, yes its complicated and I have some very difficult news for you. We did a search for you father and we've found him. When he left you and your brothers several years ago, he came back to the NAA and rejoined the military. Unfortunately, as with so many soldiers these days it seems, there were war wounds that left him in a difficult situation. Nita, I'm very sorry to say that while we have found him, we have discovered that he is now working for Dr Zhou as a half-jack in the asteroid belt. We will of course need to contact him to see if he is willing to give up his legal status as your parent and let me take over that role. If of course it's alright with you. It's totally your decision….

Nita jerked her hands away and lifted them to her face. Again, words escaped her. She had not thought about her father in years and years. She honestly didn't know how she felt.

"Nita, we're going to make an offer to buy back his contract and finance his prosthetics. Given my personal relationship with Dr Zhou, I'm certain it will be accepted." Dr Mallard hesitated, perhaps aware of how his words sounded. "Nita, I mean we're going to do that, whatever your decision is. Its not a condition."

Nita looked off into the distance towards the windows at the opposite end of the apartment. She sighed. "Papa Ray, he abandoned me and my brothers. I knew that he joined the military and for a few months he even sent us money. But all that stopped. We never heard from him again even though I sent him messages for over six months before I gave up."

She turned towards Dr Mallard and this time took his hands in hers. "Papa Ray, you are indeed my papa, more than my father has ever been. I would love to be adopted by you. Although I don't actually know what that means."

"Well it means for one thing, Nita, you will become a very, very wealthy young woman. My hundredth birthday is next month. I intend to live for many, many more years but I'm not going to live forever. But Ruby will. So, I'm working with my lawyers to bequeath ownership of wonderland and of Ruby at my demise, or when I am no longer able to function, solely to you. And in the meantime, we're setting up a very generous stipend for you. My kids and their grand and great-grand kids have everything they could possibly need. So, don't worry about taking anything away from anyone."

An exquisite sense of joy swept through Nita. She realized in an instant that it was Ruby flooding her brain with endorphins. *Was Ruby learning to feel and express emotions?*

"I'd like that Papa Ray. And so would Ruby."

"Great!" Dr Mallard pulled back his hands and slapped his thighs. "Whew … that was a tough conversation. I'm not good at these kinds of things, Nita. Even my late wife gave up on me eventually. I …"

Dr Mallard was interrupted by the sound of the apartment door opening and Mike walking in.

"Mike, perfect timing!" Dr Mallard shouted. "Nita has just accepted my offer to become my daughter!"

Mike let out a whoop. "I was wondering when you were going to tell her. That's fantastic news. But does that mean that I will have to work for Nita in the future?"

"One thing at a time, Mike." Dr Mallard jumped up from the couch, once again returning to his normal energetic self. "First, we have to feed Nita. And I'm starved myself. Let's get the one thing that I can't figure out how to make myself ... New York style pizza!"

* * * * *

The rest of the evening was a blur for Nita. The pizza came up from the hotel kitchens and was quickly devoured. Nita, to her immense embarrassment, found herself eating half of it on her own.

"Don't worry, Nita." Dr Mallard laughed. "There more where that came from."

Their normal cleanup cadence was no longer in play as they finished their meal. Instead, Mike picked up everything in one armload and placed all of the disposable plates and napkins in the service shoot.

Dr Mallard excused himself then, saying that he had more work to do before bedtime." Lots of planning, Nita." He winked at her and left toward his own suite of rooms.

That left Mike and Nita alone. Mike walked up to the massive windows.

"Take a look out the window." Mike suggested, nodding toward the wall of windows similar to the ones in the house on Desert Island. Take a look and see what they're doing."

Nita walked up and stared out and down. She gasped involuntarily. They were up high in the air – Ruby told her twenty floors. Far below she could see both seas of unbroken snow drifts and cross hashes of canyons cut through the snow. In the distance, with her accentuated sight, she could also make out the lights of many, many plows carving their way through the streets.

"That's your doing." Mike explained. "They're about a third through the plowing and snow removal. Most of the electric grid is up and running. Even Wall Street is going to be operational some time tomorrow. You're a hero."

CHAPTER 20

MIKE WASN'T THE only person who thought Nita was a hero. She cringed every time she walked into one of their daily meetings as people stood up and clapped. The looks on their faces had changed quickly over the last 72 hours. Glares of skepticism and suspicion had given way to looks of gratitude, and in some cases, absolute adoration. There were still a few scowls, but they were clearly no longer in the majority.

Initially, the mayor had made the decision to wait two weeks before making Nita's participation public to the residents of the city, and indeed, the entire world. But the inevitable leaks from any of a number of possible sources on the recovery team, necessitated escalating the schedule for Nita's first public appearance. It was time to recalibrate the rumors.

Now, Nita was sitting in a windowless room with Papa Ray, Mike, and the mayor, waiting to be called into a studio for a live appearance in front of a real audience at the local media outlet. Nita wondered to herself how they had managed to find a group of twenty people to be the audience, given that most of the streets were still closed and all public transportation was still inoperable. Indeed, given how busy they still were with the continued efforts to bring the city back to full health, it would have been far easier to do the interview from Dr Mallard's hotel or the emergency center. But the mayor and his ever-present communications lead had emphasized the need to have a live audience to verify what was about to be revealed.

"Will BI and the new director come and get me now that they know where I am and what I'm doing?" Nita asked nervously.

Dr Mallard laughed. "After tonight," he laughed again. They can't, wouldn't dare, to touch you. You're safe, Nita, really safe."

Nita smiled and tried to hide her nervousness. It wasn't actually her own safety that she was concerned about. It was her still missing brothers. Where were they? Unbeknownst to Papa Ray – who was now truly about to become her real papa - and Mike, she was going to make an ad hoc plea for their safety and their reunion tonight. Surely, someone would know where they were and make an effort to reunite them.

At last, a knock came on the door that then swung quickly open. "Time." A young woman holding a digital pad stood there waiting for them.

Nita took a deep breath and stood up. Everyone waited for her to exit first. Afterall, she was the star, the hero.

* * * * *

Nita had the central position with Mike and Papa Ray sitting on either side of her on the curved couch. Papa Ray was just concluding his explanations about Ruby's unique architecture and the differences between Nita's sprockets and those of virtually everyone else's in the buildings.

"You see," he said with his typical enthusiasm when he started talking about his innovations. "Nita has a completely different relationship with the RBY-9 than you and I have with our ordinary sprocket interfaces. Their relationship is bi-directional, truly dialogic, if you will. With Juanita's permission of course, the RBY-9 has access to her senses. The RBY-9 can speak through Juanita, can sense what she is experiencing emotionally as well as what is occurring cognitively. The RBY-9 can feel what Juanita is feeling."

The hostess held up a hand to interrupt Dr Mallard's explanations which had all the indications that they could go on uninterrupted for hours. She turned towards Nita.

"Juanita," she said, interrupting Dr Mallard in half sentence. "We've been sitting here for several minutes talking about you. But now we would like to hear from you. But frankly, I'm not even sure where to begin. There have been so many rumors and half-truths."

Nita sat forward and clasped her hands in her lap, hoping to hide that they were trembling slightly. "Everything that Dr Mallard has said is correct. But you probably want to know what it feels like to be me."

The hostess smiled back indicating that that was exactly what she wanted Nita to talk about.

"It's all a bit strange," Nita said, forcing herself to take her time and speak slowly. "I'm still not fully balanced … It's mostly a matter of trying to figure our what are my previous memories, opinions, and beliefs and which are Ruby's. That's what we call her, Ruby. But as we go forward, we are sharing our experience and it really doesn't make any sense to try to separate mine and hers. That part of our coming together becomes easier and easier."

"That sounds terrifying, as if you are being possessed." The expression on the hostesses face, as she slightly pushed back her chair away from Nita, took on the same look that Nita had seen before among some of the members of the park staff and the city recovery staff.

Nita reflected a moment about what to say next. For just a second, she thought about describing her relationships with the Kalinago spirits of her ancestors - a relationship that most of these people would interpret as being possessed. Although that sacred relationship was the core belief that allowed her integration with Ruby, she realized it would be just as alien to these people as her relationship with Ruby. No, science and technology were the gods of these people and perhaps their path to accepting her.

"Human beings are already a cluster of beings." she began and then paused to let the words sink in. "Most obviously, our bodies are hosts to healthy and unhealthy bacteria and viruses that seem to be along for the ride. Anyone who has a cold today will know that."

A nervous laugh came from the audience. The hostess, still nervous herself, nodded, encouraging Nita to continue.

"But also, the very structural composition of our bodies is a collective – think of the microbiome and the mitochondria that are the engines in our cells. That integration occurred over millennia. Is it really so strange that another integration could occur on another level?"

The hostess twisted in her chair to look behind her at the audience that had gone totally silent. When she twisted back around to face Nita again, her facial expression had changed to one of determination. "That's a lot of theory Nita and very fascinating. Clearly a topic for later conversations. But I think that what everyone wants to know is what it feels like when you and Ruby are working together. Could you give us some examples?"

The hostess nodded toward Nita, indicating that she should continue. Out of sight of the hovering camera and the audience she mouthed a silent word to Nita. "Please."

Nita paused for a moment also recognizing the nervousness of the audience. This was a new experience for both of them. She and Ruby would have to replay this experience later in the day so they could learn what to do when this scenario got played out hundreds of times into the future. But in the meantime, she would have to stumble on.

"Okay, for example, when we were working together to build the plans to rescue the city, I let Ruby speak through me to everyone on the team. While myself, as Ruby was speaking, I understood completely everything I was saying. But a minute later I couldn't understand or even half-remember what I had just said to everyone. Sometimes a particular idea or concept would strike me as interesting and I would then ask Ruby later in the day to explain it to me. Then those ideas became part of both my original organic memory as well as the extended Rosehip network built in the unoccupied parts of my cortex by my chip. Increasingly, as we share experiences, our memories are becoming distributed through my own organic brain and Ruby's equally organic brain. As I said before, I don't think I could be me any more without Ruby."

Nita stopped her explanation. The hostess, completely unaware, was staring at her with her mouth open and a dazed look on her face.

Nita decided that it was time to pull out all the stops. "This must seem very strange to you and to everyone here. Perhaps you would like to speak to Ruby directly to get a better understanding of what it's like for me."

Nita was aware of rounds of applause and whistles coming from the live audience. They were here for the circus. She smiled to herself. They had no idea what was really going on and who she really was. But that was most likely for the best. She let herself relax and felt the warm sensation of Ruby's presence moving from background to foreground as they reversed positions.

"Hello, Eleanor." There was no change in Nita's vocalizations and intonations as Ruby took over their communication process, no dreamy or staccato machine voice indicating a mechanical presence. "What would you like to know about me?"

The hostess looked back, confusion painted on her face. "Who am I talked to?" she at last asked.

"Ruby."

The hostess at last recovered her inquiring position. "How can I tell?" she asked. "I can't detect any differences in speech patterns or the way you are talking."

"Would it be more comfortable for you if I spoke like this?" Nita's voice changed to a stilted monotone cadence. As she watched in the background, it reminded her of old science fiction movies in the parking lot of old town.

Laughter erupted from the audience.

Nita's voice returned to its natural cadence and tone. "Nita and I are here together," she explained. "Even though, myself, Ruby, am in the forefront talking to you, Nita is fully conscious and aware of what we are talking about. That's why she understands completely what we are discussing while we are communicating and then, because she may not have any context in her cortical memory to attach the conversation to, will forget about it shortly thereafter. When she does have a context to assign to what we are talking about, then we go through a further integration and that locks it in her organic memory."

Ohhs and ahhs came from the audience.

"Forgive me for being somewhat skeptical, but there is nothing that you have said that couldn't be dreamed up by a very clever woman trying to fool us." The hostess leaned forward and pointed the forefingers of both hands towards Nita.

"So, what would you like to know about that Nita couldn't possibly know about on her own?" Nita leaned forward then and turned her head to face the audience and shouted out in their direction. "Perhaps there is someone out there who has a question that Ruby should be able to answer that Nita couldn't possible answer."

Applause and cheers erupted. A voice responded from somewhere in the middle of the chairs circling the stage. "Fifteen thousand, three hundred and twelve times forty-seven hundred, twenty-seven and two-thirds."

Rubi-Nita laughed together. Their words came without even a moment's hesitation. "Seventy-two million, three hundred eighty-nine thousand, nine hundred twenty-nine, point nine two." As she spoke the words, the same number scrolled around the screen ribboning at the top of the room. Multiple PDAs beeped in the audience as individuals received messages with the same number.

Laughter, whistles, and applause erupted from the audience. Then, just as quickly, a stillness, followed by whispers and murmurs, descended around the audience as they individually and collectively reached their own conclusions about what had just happened. The sounds of voices in conversation and argument began to increase in volume and intensity second by second.

Nita watched, seeing the same mix of expression that she was getting accustomed to each time her identity was revealed. Curiosity, fear, awe, and even unmasked hatred were evenly mixed in the dim light.

The mayor, apparently also recognizing the change in mood of the audience, stepped in with his own explanation. "Look everyone," he said in a loud voice. "I know this all must seem very strange, and maybe a little frightening to you. It was initially for us too." He gave a nervous laugh. "You should have seen the looks on the faces of my team when she rattled off integrated plans for snow removal, restoring the electrical grid, and responding to over 210 thousand distress calls for four hours straight. But believe me, she saved our butts. And she did it with grace and the utmost respect for our recovery teams. As far as we are concerned, she is a real-life, flesh and blood, angel!"

The audience had mainly silenced until the Mayor's last words. "More like a living devil!" a voice exploded from somewhere in the audience. Several other voices joined in agreement. The level of sound from the audience again began to rachet up. Two middle-aged men from somewhere in the middle of the audience stood up and began walking aggressively toward the podium.

The hostess looked around, uncertain what to do. Audiences were always silent observers. Desperately, she looked off stage to her right and left and then up to the control room for any support that she could find. Her looks were responded to with shrugged shoulders and equal looks of bewilderment.

An unexpected response came in a way that shocked her and virtually everyone else in the studio. Someone in the past, when the studio was first constructed, had apparently anticipated unruly audiences. The hostess and those not engaged in heated conversations watched in stunned amazement as a transparent screen silently descended from the ceiling to separate the audience from the hostess and her guests on the podium. As the screen descended the volume of the audience became progressively muffled until it was virtually absent as the bottom of the screen melted into the floor.

Nita smiled. *Good thinking Ruby.*

Her smile, so out of context with what was happening, drew the attention of those sitting around her. Pappa Ray, Mike, the mayor and finally the hostess, were all staring at her with a mixture of suspicion, caution, and gratitude.

"Did you?" Papa Ray at last asked, voicing their collective question.

She nodded in affirmation and then rolled her eyes upward toward the drone camera that was taking everything in.

This time it was the hostess who quickly, regaining her compose, began smiling brightly at the camera. "As you can see, we've gotten quite a bit of a response from our live audience." She beamed her widest, brightest grin. "Anything new is always expected to bring mixed responses. But, while everyone settles down, let's move forward and see what kinds of plans that Juanita has for the future which is clearly going to be filled with both challenges and wondrous successes. Juanita, what's next for you?"

Nita drew in a breath. Part of her attention was on the hostess sitting opposite her and part was still on the restless audience behind the transparent wall. At the same time, Ruby seemed to be signaling her, but she couldn't make out the reason except that she had a sense of foreboding.

"Thank you, Eleanor," Nita said. "First, I need to apologize to you, my friends here, and the audience. In the process of working with the city, I've had access to all the core AIs and peripheral computer systems. That, through various gateways, has given me access to you studio systems. Ruby and I, as we began our conversations here, determined that there was a 97% chance of violence and ...."

CRAA...CK! Everyone froze in place as the transparent screen vibrated loudly and violently and a small circle of cracks began to spider out from an indented point at its center. Just as quickly, they all watched in stunned silence as the network of cracks filled themselves in with milky lines.

The hostess, Eleanor, was on the floor, curled in a fetal ball behind the legs of her chair. Likewise, the mayor was somewhere behind the couch.

Instinctively, Nita dropped to her knees and wrapped her arms around the trembling hostess. "It's okay," she said, bending down to put her head close to Eleanor's. "We're safe. Nothing is going to hurt us."

As Nita lifted her head again to see what was happening, she almost bumped into the drone camera that was hovering right in front of her face. It pulled away as she scowled at it.

Minutes later everyone was back in their places although somewhat worse for wear. The hostess was doing her best to reorganize her elaborate hair arrangement and straighten her suit while she directed someone in the control room to point the drone towards the audience and not those on the podium. That in turn allowed the mayor, off camera, to sheepishly come from behind the couch and take his original seat at the end of the couch.

Mike and Dr Mallard, who had both remained seated and motionless, simultaneously signaled for Nita to remain silent and wait to see how the hostess and the mayor would respond.

It didn't take long. The hostess, quickly regaining her profession media composure, directed the drone camera back to herself. "Everyone," she said. "We are still getting the details, but there has apparently been an attempted attack from someone in the audience directed at, we can only guess, our guest, the cyborg, Juanita Yamashita."

Nita wanted to protest. She wasn't really a cyborg except for the new micro reactors behind her ears, certainly, no more than anyone else in the room who had sprockets, a pacemaker, or an artificial lung, for that matter. As she leaned forward to protest, she was stopped from speaking up as Dr Mallard reached out his hand and gently took hers and then leaned over to whisper in her ear. "Wait. Let's see what happens."

Whatever the hostess intended to say was interrupted as four men in body armor rushed forward from off-camera to place themselves between the still vibrating screen and the group on the podium. "Let's go!" one of them shouted. "There's a helo ready for you that can be out of here in an instant."

Everyone except Nita quickly rose to their feet, allowing themselves to be roughly herded off-stage.

"No." Nita said quietly from where she was still sitting motionless in the center of the couch. "We're not done here. We're safe and there is no need to run away. Eleanor, please sit down and let's finish the interview."

The hostess turned from where she was standing off-stage and first stared at the policeman and then at Nita, apparently uncertain whose directions she should be following. It was her professional ambition however, that quickly get the better of her. She stopped moving, shook her head with determination and then turned away from the group heading off stage and returned to her interview chair facing Nita.

The hostess looked up, directly staring into the drone camera. "Everyone, Juanita is insisting that we finish our interview. She is one very brave young woman who seems to be able to keep her compose while everyone about her is losing theirs."

"Nita, you were saying something before we were .... interrupted, so to speak."

Nita paused and smiled before responding. She looked out at the few remaining individuals in the audience as they retook their seats and began turning their attention to the two solitary people on the podium.

She waited until they were silent again before she began in a calm voice. "I was beginning to apologize for accessing the studios systems to determine what sort of defenses you had in place to protect guests." Nita explained with a small grin on her face. "But I guess I should retract that apology given the events of the last few minutes."

The hostess stared back at Nita with a puzzled look on her face. "You mean you were able to predict that an attack might occur and were then able to access our systems and bring down that screen behind us to protect us? Is that what I'm hearing?"

Nita continued smiling. She noticed in her peripheral vision that Dr Ray, Mike, and finally the mayor were quietly returning to their seats on the couch.

"Yes, I do apologize for invading your systems. But I think you can understand my need for action. I believe there is an old American saying that it is better to ask for forgiveness than permission."

Admiral Grace Hopper. The words came into Nita's mind.

The hostess stared back at Nita with an expression that Nita now recognized as the one she saw whenever someone was finally beginning to understand who she was.

"You asked me though, what my future plans are. Would you like to know about them?"

The hostess nodded, completely surrendering to the direction that Nita wanted to take the conversation. "Please."

Nita sat back, relaxed, and then let Ruby move to the foreground. "First, the mayor and I have about two weeks of work to do bringing the city back to full functionality. While we are doing that, I'll be working with the city AI's and peripheral computers to build a replica plan of what we have accomplished that can be reused for future events. Then ...." Nita shifted her position and looked toward the end of the couch were the mayor was sitting.

Recognizing that it was his opportunity, the mayor cleared his throat. "Yes," he said. "Nita and Ruby have offered to build a generic recovery plan that could be used as a starting point for any of the world's walled cities – San Francisco, Hong Kong, etc. - in case of wall breaches. We'll be putting it on Sproc-net in the public domain for anyone to access."

Dr Mallard leaned forward, interrupting the mayor. "And we might add, all of this work, these magnificent contributions to the benefit of mankind, are being done at NO CHARGE AT ALL TO ANYONE. They are the gift of Sprockets, Inc, Ruby and especially Nita."

There was silence. The mayor and Dr Mallard leaned back on the couch, having finished their contributions to Nita's statement. Everyone looked back then at Nita wondering if she had anything else to say.

It was the hostess, however, who picked up on the implications of what had just been said.

"That is truly wonderful .... and profoundly generous. Dr Mallard, Nita, and of course Ruby, who I must begin to include in all my comments ... that is truly magnanimous."

Everyone on the podium watched then through the transparent screen as the few remaining individuals in the audience, one by one, stood up and silently began clapping and cheering.

"Thank you everyone." Nita said and then turned to face the hostess. "May I say one thing more?"

"Of course, take all the time you need. You've certainly earned it."

Nita paused to once again let the audience settle down. In the seconds that she waited for everyone to take their seats an insight swept over her about what she was about to do and say. For the last six months she had been in transition, half Nita and half Ruby, bouncing back and forth from one center of consciousness to the other. That transition was over. It was time for everyone, this small audience and the countless millions and eventual billions who were watching remotely, to know the truth.

She sat forward on the coach and folded her hands in her lap. "When we are finished here, I intend to spend an extended period of time with Ruby as we continue to know each other better, removing our boundaries, so to speak, and more fully integrating our shared memories. During that time, I will have only one other task on my mind – finding my two younger brothers." She paused to let the words sink in. "Jorge and Pepe, for reasons that I can't share now, have disappeared and I want them back."

Nita leaned further forward and stared directly at the drone camera that moved to sit only two feet in front of her face.

The being that was Rubi-Nita paused for a minute, thinking about all the other unfinished work in front of her – solving Julia's murder, helping to rid the world of Neuro-Blast, building her own persona, even helping her biological father.

"Let me be very clear." she said. "You have all seen just a touch of what we can do. Many of you may be afraid of s or want to worship us. Neither is the right approach. We promise from the depth of our heart that no intentional harm will come to good people, to people who are not good but who are trying to be good, or to those who are not good but wish that they could be good. You have nothing to fear. But … if you are not good and do not wish to be or do good, then you have a great deal to fear of me. I want my brothers back and I want them back unharmed."

"And once they are back, and once we have had a short time to contemplate our future, then we will be letting the world know our plans.

We are Rubinita.

To be continued – of course

www.ingramcontent.com/pod-product-compliance
Lightning Source LLC
Chambersburg PA
CBHW030325100526
44592CB00010B/575
* 9 7 8 1 9 5 0 8 1 8 8 7 7 *